Trading Your Facade
for Authentic Life

The

WOMAN
Behind the Mask

Jan Coleman

Kregel
Publications

Library of Congress Cataloging-in-Publication Data
Coleman, Jan.
   The woman behind the mask: trading your facade for authentic life / by Jan Coleman.
       p.   cm.
   Includes bibliographical references.
   1. Christian women—Religious life I. Title.
BV4844.C653   2006   248.8'43—dc22   2005032479

ISBN 0-8254-2405-4

Contents

Preface

Before we utter our first words we learn to playact. Then we grow up and most of us leave the pretending behind, but some of us never do. We keep putting on a show, and it's second nature now. We hide behind our facades and give the impression that we've got everything under control so no one will suspect our deepest secrets, doubts, and fears.

I've been there behind the mask, and it's a stifling place to be.

Since being a Broadway star was my first big dream, I've chosen the stage theme for this book. Oh, the content is nothing new. You've heard these same principles before, but often a new twist on old truths will bring new understanding.

Thanks for joining me for a while, and I trust it's because you have your heart set on a leading role in the Divine Drama, the one you alone were destined to play. God has a script written for you, and he wants to go into rehearsal for the most important part you'll ever play—the real, authentic you.

In *Hamlet,* Shakespeare wrote, "To thine own self be true." The worst thing we can do is betray ourselves and the God who made us, and be less than we were designed to be.

It's been said that you teach what you need to learn, so the following pages contain things I still wrestle with as a woman and Christ follower.

There is no magic formula. I'm not one of those authors who breaks things down into bullet points and top-ten tips. I'm a storyteller—I share from my own and others' experiences—and hopefully together we can identify some of the beliefs and dynamics that have been running your life. Things you might want to change. I hope this book inspires you to partner with God for the abundant life. It's yours, and it's waiting for you.

One size does not fit all with this program, either. Your journey to wholeness will not mirror mine. God designs our spiritual conditioning, our healing of past hurts, in a way that fits how he has wired us.

I say "we" often. Yes, I'm generalizing, and with some of it you'll shake your head—*that's not me*—but writing this way helps me think of you as a friend and picture us sitting in my back yard, sipping apricot iced tea on the outdoor wicker set I bought at a discount at the end of last summer. We're laughing and crying and being genuine with each other.

As I share my stories I'll be challenging you to a new way of thinking, to let go of the props and facades that have no purpose and place anymore. And as you move across the stage of life, Jesus will display his skill as the Great Director of your story. And as you share who you really are, others will be inspired to audition for the Greatest Show on Earth.

So let's light up the stage and begin.[†]

[†] Names marked with an asterisk (*) have been changed for privacy purposes.

Act 1

The Stage Is Set

It's opening night, and the curtain goes up on act 1. We are introduced to our main character and her world. Enter our leading lady, cast in the role of every woman: wife, mother, career professional. One hand grips the purse strings while the other manages her portfolio, and she can still push the stroller while she phones home before stopping at the market. Walking across the stage, she is cool, confident, and in control, but then something happens—in script talk we call it the inciting incident—and it throws her off-kilter. She tumbles and bumps her head. She feels faint. And somehow she knows this day in her life will be different from any other.

In the next scene she is dreaming. She is an old woman looking back on her life with regret, wondering why she swallowed the myth that she could be everything and have everything, if she worked hard enough. Now, time is short and none of it matters. "I played too many roles not intended for me," she laments. "I fooled myself by my own masquerade."

She wonders, "When did I start hiding my insecurities lest I seem weak or unstable? When did I begin collecting my parade of masks?" Now she has a closet full: some from pain and fear of rejection, others from a need for approval and the guilt from not measuring up. And the one with the devout look for Sundays. So many years of settling for saintly smiles, surface talk, and shallow relationships.

"I missed out on who God intended me to be."

She awakes with a strong desire to come out from behind her masks and be real.

Lord, help me find the woman behind the mask. Make me into someone defined by you and not by the world or my unrealistic expectations. Remove from me anything that stands between me and authentic life with you.

By the end of act 1 our leading lady is taking action; she invites the living God to be her Stage Manager, to direct her thoughts, words, attitudes, and actions. And this time, there is no turning back.

Chapter 1

Charades and Masquerades

The genuine life is not a masked ball.

Nothing between us and God, our faces shining with the brightness of his face. (2 Corinthians 3:18 MSG)

After jotting down a few notes, the counselor peered at me over her gold rimmed half-glasses. "Why don't you leave Jenny home next week and come by yourself?"

Excuse me—don't you get it? I'm here because my thirteen-year-old needs help. She just spent three days in juvenile hall. I need some biblical advice, and you're a Christian counselor. Please tell me you can fix her.

I didn't know it then—twenty-plus years ago—but God had something else in mind: he wanted to fix me first.

Curious and still desperate for some answers, I arrived the following Thursday with the familiar lump in my throat at being in Placerville again. Karen's office, tucked up in an old brick building on historic Main Street, sat across from the county courthouse where my supposed-to-be-forever marriage met its legal demise a few short months before.

Placerville was never a happy destination for me, but by the time I climbed the stairs, I had fashioned my sunniest smile.

9

After the warm-up chitchat, Karen shot straight from her shoulder pads. "Jan, you have no idea who you really are, you've been playing so many different roles in your life."

And clearly she didn't mean my passion for acting or my short-lived career on stage in high school and college.

As a child, I loved playacting and collected props and costumes—crazy hats and cowboy boots, silk gowns and satin ballet slippers—and on most summer weekends you could find me and the neighborhood gang producing variety shows in my garage. What could be more fun than pretending? We could explore, play, and make-believe.

A slight problem—I never quite grew out of it.

Karen hit the mark. Right then a quote by my favorite funny philosopher, Ashleigh Brilliant, flashed before me: "Success for some people depends on being known. For others it depends on never being found out."[1]

Ouch. This counselor seemed bent on tearing off my masks and was not about to be fooled by the one I came in wearing. Okay, that's what I get for coming back for a second helping of her, I thought, and cringed at the realization that the longer I sat in the hot seat, the more she would expose my weaknesses. I had a seismic urge to bolt for the door.

"You play the part and pretend you have it all together," she continued. *But it's all a disguise, because let's face it, on the inside I'm a mess.*

My thoughts spooled back to my childhood and act 1 of my personal drama. A respectable Bay Area family, happy and successful on the outside, but it was all window dressing, a false front. Behind closed doors, we were the cast in an ongoing soap opera playing our well-rehearsed roles and pretending very well. Every few months Daddy would whisper to me, "Mother's a bit *under the weather* tonight, dear."

Under the influence, you mean. And the bouts could last for a week or two at a time. But my modus operandi (MO) was to dodge and disregard the truth and act like it never happened. And it worked. Wrapped in my fantasies, I could keep sane. You may have come from a family like this where you just didn't air your dirty laundry, even among yourselves. Where you danced around the real stuff. My friend calls it the elephant under the rug that everybody pretends isn't there.

My school counselors didn't probe, and there were no support groups to affirm that others have this problem too, and no, you aren't crazy. While my dad seemed to cope with the unpredictability of our life, confusion reigned in this girl. Deep down I wondered, could this be my fault somehow? I covered up my insecurities and loneliness by becoming a crackerjack impersonator, imitating a girl with no insecurities.

I wore so many costumes I lost my original identity.

I hungered to fit in with the crowd. When scholastic testing revealed that I should be in the "gifted" program, I turned up my nose. Those were the brains, the geeks, the weird kids. No thanks. But my parents plopped me in there anyway, so how did I respond? By being a cut-up and not living up to my potential. Gifted was not normal, not in those days, so I masked it. I concealed my love for learning, certain it would never bring me acceptance.

The "clown" mask lasted through my high school years. My public image became a cozy and comfortable facade, especially through a traumatic youth and a testy marriage that began at age nineteen. The more problems, the brighter my mask, because I had to prove my parents were wrong when they predicted disaster.

People lauded me and my sweetheart as the perfect couple, so full of vitality and fun. Always a party at our house, and what adorable little girls we had. In truth, my deceptions were suffocating me, and I never confided in anyone that all was not as it seemed. I kept up the facade because (1) that's what I was trained to do, and (2) I loved him with everything I had.

But those were unstable years of never knowing when he'd step out on me again, then beg for another chance. Over and over I forgave him and trusted his promises. Fifteen years later, to my complete surprise, he left us, and suddenly my disguises were useless.

Everybody now knew my marriage was a flop.

When my husband snuck out the backdoor, Christ came in the front through a stranger who gave me my life Scripture verse: "I will restore to you the years that the . . . locust has eaten" (Joel 2:25 NKJV). As I relate in my first book, *After the Locusts,* she spoke in words this country girl could grasp—an onslaught of bugs devouring my carefully tended crops—and I finally got the message.

My mate had abandoned me—with two girls, forty chickens, five goats, two horses, and six pigs—but God would never leave me. He wanted my heart, and if I gave it to him, he would replant the barren fields of my ruined dreams and show me the way to true happiness.

I accepted the invitation, and God went to work on my injured soul. And for a sweet while we had a love affair, Jesus and me, with my heart singing as I reveled in my new role as the bride of Christ. I wondered, Why couldn't I have found you sooner, Lord?

The practical realities quenched my passion: finding a job to support my girls, refereeing their skirmishes, trying to detour them from self-destruction, and jockeying through legal battles trying to save the homestead from a quick divorce sale before I was ready.

Suddenly, I found myself cast in the Parable of the Sower in Matthew 13. I played the seed that fell on rocky places, the one who heard and received the Word with joy, but she had no sturdy root and her joy was oh-so brief. Along comes trouble, and she is one wilted wildflower.

Masking the Real Me

"You've survived a lot in your young life," Karen said, bringing me back to the present, "but somewhere, you lost who you were meant to be. You've masked the real you."

Now, masks were nothing new to this born thespian. They're worn as a part of a costume or a disguise, but some masks are necessary. We need them—like those worn when you play the catcher in the game to protect your face from a wild pitch. We have a closet filled with masks of every size and color, one for every illusion we want to create. One for our loved ones, another for work, and one very proper one for Sunday. And we change masks so fast in our lightning speed world that we often forget to ask, "Who am I behind this mask?"

Hey, maybe I don't want to know.

The word *act* comes from the Latin word *actus,* which means "to do." Put on an act, behave like someone else. And we've all done it. But Jesus calls us "to be," *to have reality.* It's the root word of "belong." Belong to God and ourselves.

We can catch on to the first part, but the next one trips us up sometimes because being natural doesn't always come naturally. Legendary entertainer Sophie Tucker might never have found her true identity if it weren't for a flub-up. As a child performing in amateur shows, Sophie became an audience favorite as "the fat girl" because by age thirteen, she already weighed one hundred forty-five pounds. Later on, she was offered a small slot in a production on one condition: she appear in blackface because she was so big and ugly. As the story goes, she tried unsuccessfully to scrap her blackface act, so when her costumes and makeup failed to arrive in time for a show one night, she took a risk and went on without her disguise.

And guess what? She was an instant hit and never wore it again. Before long, she was the Red Hot Mama, and instead of being ashamed of her looks, she capitalized on them. The audience loved hearing her make fun of herself.

So this lady became a huge success by accident, by accepting and liking herself.

Our society—Christianity included—is like a masked ball where we are invited to come as somebody else, to hide behind the illusion we want to create. Many of us fake being good Christians, and it works for the short run. We claim God's promises in public and keep our doubts very private. Then something happens, a crisis like a divorce or a death or a daughter landing in juvenile hall, and we reach a defining moment. We either run to God and his truth or run away from him in pursuit of a fast fix on our own. It's our survival instinct kicking in.

An e-mail from Laura after she read my first book describes this well: "My husband and I were in full-time music ministry. Our dream was to record songs for God's glory. We had two precious boys and on the surface it looked like we had the dream life, not so behind closed doors. Our ministry was a sham. I started drinking to numb the pain of my husband's affairs. Then I was faced with the threat of cancer to the throat which marked the beginning of the end of my lies. The story is so intricate and detailed, but my marriage ended and I'm teaching piano as my livelihood. I don't want to 'play church' anymore. I want to live the life."

Laura came to the end of her masquerade where she longed to embrace what's real and authentic. All those years laboring to cover up the dark secrets of her family life drained her emotionally dry and took a toll on her physical health. That's where I found myself that day in Karen's office, still smiling on the outside but sporting a hidden grudge against the Lord for my predicaments—after all, he allowed all these things to happen to me—and I longed for my reward, right now. A heavenly Oscar with Jan's name on it: Best Performance in a Difficult Role.

I still kept up the act, appearing to be the joyful growing Christian to everyone—especially my parents who turned a skeptical eye on their born-again daughter—so no one would guess my secret. I had begun to wonder about this commitment I made; becoming a Christ follower is a tad bit more than raising hands at a camp bonfire and a simple decision between heaven and hell. Christianity is a totally new lifestyle, and not an easy one at that. I kept wondering, how hard must I try to please God? And what guarantees do I have that he'll come through on his promises for me while I'm in the prime years of my womanhood?

A few months prior I attended a seminar on basic life principles, covering topics like the wounded spirit, resolving childhood hurts, and general explanations of living God's way. The speaker talked about divorce and remarriage, and bottom line, it seemed I was supposed to remain single forever.

Here I was a new believer, eager to understand this Christian thing and do it right, and I hear this man in front of thousands of people announcing that I, unwillingly single—must remain that way. Not only can I never remarry, he said, but if my unbelieving spouse has tied the knot—which he was about to do—my chief purpose in life is to pray for his new marriage.

Whoops. See Jan put her pen away and check out. I don't recall anything else the man said from then on. My bruised heart couldn't take it, and I didn't understand that God would resolve all my questions as I walked in faith with him. I drove home thinking, *if this is the way it is, then perhaps I made an error in joining up with a God who would condemn me to a prayer closet with a life-sized poster of my husband and my replacement.*

Not this chick. Not happening. No way. Years later I heard that this seminar speaker has changed his position a bit and cut some slack for those injured parties like me married to and abandoned by unbelievers. I don't know, but possibly he got wind of the way some people reacted to this, by running away from God, like I did.

So I donned my dancing shoes and went out looking for some attention, finding it in a big broad shoulder to rest my hurting head upon while love songs played. The big shoulder hung around for quite a while too, fooled by my mask. And it was so easy to wear it with him, to forget my troubles on the dance floor. He thought I was just fine and ready for a "growing friendship."

And I was heaps of fun, if I do say so myself, but as Pastor Bill, now retired and a gentleman rancher, once told me, "You've got to get a hold of yourself before you can get a hold of a man."

The have-it-all-together act could not go on forever.

Setting Up for a Spiritual Makeover

So on that red-letter day in Karen's office many years ago, I sensed the gig was over. God led me to Karen, an insightful woman who dared to ask the definitive questions: Did I have the courage to give up the game, to grow up the lost child, to find the freedom of who I was meant to be and live in the truth of the risen Christ? Could I trust him with my whole being, trust the Holy Spirit to reveal in his time and with his methods that in shedding the masks comes freedom? Masks gone, I would be able to see myself in a new, untarnished light, untainted by my own misunderstanding.

Socrates, after being found guilty of heresy, said this to his jurors in Athens: The unexamined life is not worth living. To this ancient philosopher, the pursuit of truth of the soul is our highest calling. Merely living is not enough; it must be authentic. This may be what Jeremiah meant when he said, "Let us examine our ways and test them, and let us return to the LORD" (Lam. 3:40).

The faith life is a continual searching inside, taking a good honest look at ourselves. How many times do we take the Lord's Supper and hear a paraphrase of 1 Corinthians 11:28, "Examine your motives, test your heart, come to this meal in holy awe" (MSG).

Examine my motives, that's what I wanted to do. But I'm no dummy.

I knew the program meant pain, and lots of it. Some of my masks were attached with superglue. I felt myself grinding my teeth.

To top it off, Karen said, "God is not concerned with making you happy right now, Jan, but making you complete, one with him, and that means it may get a bit uncomfortable."

You have to chuckle at her understatements. Giving up the old me would mean major torment, I could count on that. It's no secret that God uses pain to prod us into change, but we don't exactly roll out the red carpet and welcome it, do we? Rather, we resist change until we hit one of those defining moments, a pivotal moment in the story, when we suddenly get it. We recognize that the pain of staying the same will ultimately be worse than the pain of changing.

There you have a snapshot of me that day, standing under the "Enlist Here" sign for the spiritual makeover program, longing to part company with my old role, throw away the masks, and let my true face shine. The part I'd written for myself in the drama of life just wasn't working. God the Author would create a role scripted for me and be my Divine Director.

Just put yourself in his hands, Jan.

Sometimes, no matter how much it hurts to stay stuck, we shut the door to our heart and hang up the "Do Not Disturb" sign.

I remember when Patti* first called me a year or so ago. It was a memorable day because I was in the midst of cleaning my refrigerator—which doesn't happen often—when the phone rang. She had just finished *After the Locusts* and had never called an author before. Leaving the leftovers and limp vegetables on the counter, I spent an hour on the phone as she poured out her heart over a disintegrating marriage to a cruel and abusive man. Raised in a mainline Protestant church, she was visiting the Unity church and "searching for truth," so, she had some questions.

"They're nice, warm people," she said, "but, there are no real answers."

Our church has a motto of "real help for real people," and I knew our pastor's practical message that Sunday would speak to her confusion, and since she lived just a half-hour away I invited her to join me on Sunday. "Let's meet at LaBou for breakfast," I suggested since it's my second "office" in town. After ordering our lattes, Patti said, "Well, I'm not feeling well and can't make it to church. I wanted to meet you anyway, to thank you for taking time with me."

Trying to maintain composure, she admitted, "Jan, I'm just faking it," and I could see that her emotional seams were ripping apart.

"I can't let anybody know what's really going on," she added. "Not my work or my kids. I don't know what to do. I'm so afraid of being alone."

Oh what a familiar story: God on the pursuit, woman on the run. "I'm afraid of confronting my anger, afraid of losing control, afraid to let go of my old self," she said.

"I know, Patti. You can trust God with your honest feelings, just as you're trusting me." Since she already knew my story from reading my book, she sought me out to hear the truth, which I offered. Saving the marriage wasn't the real issue. God's spirit was drawing her to him. "Let Jesus into your heart and make it new."

She nodded. The truth resonated with her, and I could see the longing, sense the hunger in her spirit for authentic life. "Can I have a rain check on church?" she asked. "I'll meet you next week, definitely."

But when Sunday came around so did another phone call and another excuse. Over the following weeks we had some candid conversations as she updated me on her continuing drama, but she didn't respond to my messages at all. While her pain led her to me, she recognized that to change would be painful and the fear of the unknown was just too much. Fear of changing the way she coped with her situation and the shame of the truth kept her from exploring the God who heals. As painful as the masked life is, there is an odd comfort in going back to the same old patterns.

Patti chose to paper over the cracks one more time, slip back behind the mask, and falsely hope for the best.

The first requirement to enlist in God's makeover program is guts. I call it pluck because I like the sound of that word. It has a kick to it, a zest. Pluck has little to do with luck; it's a healthy desire to rise above our worst self.

The apostle Paul describes the program well in Ephesians 4. "Everything—and I do mean everything—connected with that old way of life has to go. . . . Get rid of it! And then take on an entirely new way of life—a God-fashioned life, a life renewed from the inside and working itself into your conduct as God accurately reproduces his character in you" (vv. 22–24 MSG).

I don't know about you, but the God-fashioned life has a sweet sound to me. Dumping the distractions, all the false beliefs about God's character and our own, releasing the burdens that stand between us and the full life Christ promises.

It's what the Bible calls burning away the dross: "Take away the dross from the silver, and the smith has material for a vessel" (Prov. 25:4 RSV). Just another word for the sludge and scum that isn't visible to the naked eye, but floats to the top after the heat's cranked up. And only the Master can do it. When Jesus heals a heart, restores a soul, or revives a relationship, he never does it halfway. He's an all-out God, and Jesus is in the remaking business. Given free access to the deep regions of our soul, he will finish his work and uncover our true worth so we can show the world who he is.

We get tunnel vision when it comes to understanding what it means to be spiritual. We think we can function as a Bible study leader or Sunday school teacher, attend the weekly prayer meetings and fast one day a week, even lead others to Christ, then slip our phobias and family problems under the carpet.

But they keep trying to crawl out.

The Christian life is an integrated life—physical, mental, emotional, spiritual—and involves the whole person. And one thing I know for certain, you cannot be spiritually mature and stay emotionally deficient. Not going to happen. Oh sure, you can order your devout and saintly mask from the masquerade shop and fool some of the people, some of the time.

The author of Hebrews urged Christians to move out of their comfort zones and digest the deeper knowledge of God, to stop trying to blend into the culture. Milk is for beginners, he tells them; solid food is for the mature (Heb. 5:11–6:1). A strong warning against salvation by self-help.

If we want authentic life let's return to the basics of who we are in Christ—his chosen children—and let him expose our wrong attitudes and motives. Paul reminds us in 1 Corinthians that "the Spirit searches all things, even the deep things of God" (2:10). If we give him permission, he will root out the deceptions that have steered us off course.

I came to the point where I wanted God to grow me into someone more like himself. I was a poor likeness of anybody—and least of all, any of my masks. The Lord was about to ask me, "May I have those? You won't be needing them anymore."

So true, and as Solomon reminds us, there is nothing new under the sun (Eccl. 1:9). There are no missing pieces yet to be discovered. We have the timeless truth at our fingertips, tucked in the Bibles we carry to church. And we have as examples the company of those who've journeyed to wholeness, evidence that the effort is worth whatever price we pay.

We're all seeking to find our life's purpose. Why do books like Rick Warren's *The Purpose Driven Life* fly off the shelves? Because we're all trying to make sense of our existence, but it's critical we pursue the purpose with intention and determination, not casual indifference.

In Karen's office long ago, my options were clear. I could stop driving aimlessly in the valley of defeat, no more cruising through the land of coping. There was such a thing as abundant life, and I wanted it. Yes, God accepts us just as we are—masks and all—but he loves us so much, he won't let us stay there.

You may be one of those reality show junkies hooked on programs like *Extreme Makeover: Home Edition*, one of the most talked about shows on prime-time TV as I write this book. A rundown house, a deserving family, a seven-day makeover. Walls moved, floors replaced, facades radically changed. I see a spiritual connection. The crew comes in to redeem an existing structure. They give it a total transformation.

If you come away with only one thing from this book, my hope is that you welcome this thing called transformation. A complex word for sure. And to seize the meaning of words, I always check my thesaurus for synonyms, this time coming up with *reshape, change for the better,* and *change the face of.*

Isn't that what transformation is? An unveiling, an unmasking.

Look what Paul says about removing the veils (or masks if you will): ". . . so that we can be mirrors that brightly reflect the glory of the Lord. And as the Spirit of the Lord works within us, we become more and more like him and reflect his glory even more" (2 Cor. 3:18 NLT).

Everyone wants to be transformed in some way or another, and whether we find our transformation in the truth or not depends on where we start our search. Last year I read that the pop star Madonna, the Material Girl, was planning a name change. Intent on a new image, she's vowed to put her wild days behind her, so she opted for the name *Esther,* after the biblical queen.

Raised a Catholic, Madonna was first named for her mother who died young. On a 20/20 program last year, she said, "I want to attach myself to an energy of a different name."[2]

You can't get a better name than Esther; she's my idea of the authentic woman—but I wonder where Madonna's search will take her. Will she ever turn to the true energy source, the name above all names? Jesus, Lord and King, the Savior, the Sower, our Beloved, the Refiner, Redeemer, Restorer, and Rebuilder.

He died for all of us, for the old life we used to live and the abundant life we're promised to have.

Unmasking the Real Me

Maybe peace like a river is just a perky little camp song to you, but not a reality. In my travels speaking to women's groups, I hear so many stories: broken relationships, abuse, a bad diagnosis, sudden tragic losses, wayward children. So many gals I meet are trapped in guilt and regret, replaying their foul-ups nonstop in their head. Others are permanently disillusioned with a life that's hard to bear, or a mate with high standards and a condemning scowl. So they learn to stay silent, to keep the peace.

That's what some of us were taught to do.

So many women are keeping their true face, their true identity and feelings masked. As Beth Moore says in her book *Believing God* about why we hide, "They think, 'If people really knew I'm struggling with this . . . or I have this temptation or that, they would think I'm a terrible person and I can't get my spiritual life together.'"[3]

We fear that if people could see what's really going on they may judge or criticize us. So we frantically create a mask to hide behind, a facade that aids us in pretending, shields us from a glance that might penetrate to reality.

We wonder, What if we bare our souls and someone takes advantage of our vulnerability? That's scary. To reveal too much of our true selves is to give others power over us. You may have been betrayed by a friend or loved one, even a business partner, and ask yourself, Who can I trust anymore? It's safer to hide out.

Maybe it's a secret sin, shame, or fear that threatens. We cling to those masks like Eve clung to her fig leaf.

You may be playing the role of the contented woman but something inside you is ready to burst, some new frontier that's calling and it won't let go, and this is a defining moment. You want to break loose and try something new, but you have to overcome the fear. Or maybe you are trapped in the busyness of daily life—it may even be the work of God—but you've lost the deep intimacy with your King and want to get it back.

Have you ever spent so much time on your persona that you neglect your character? Take it from me, persona is the imitation; it's what we plaster on the outside. Character is the real thing fashioned from God's unchanging truth. It's what we wear on the inside and it works itself into every choice we make.

The genuine woman, the one God designed for a glorious purpose, may be hidden under many facades, and it might be like removing Russian nesting dolls from within each other until one clearly stands alone and unique.

The one that looks exactly like you.

Whatever is between you and a vibrant relationship with the living God is a mask—a barrier—that needs to be removed. And you may have no idea what that is at this point, and that's okay. There may be things inside you that are so frightening that they're buried in your subconscious. Just as in a courtship, we are hesitant to reveal our secrets until we're secure in the intentions of the one we will risk loving. We must trust before we can lay bare our truest self.

God waits and keeps pulling you toward him with the magnet of his love, a love that wants to make you over from the inside out. And his touch might arrive from a direction you never expected—a book, a seminar, a friend, a counselor.

Like me, you may have been piling on the masks for years, and you've

give it over

played so many roles, you're not sure which one is you. Becoming an authentic woman means separating ourselves from the roles we play in life; by going beneath the persona to find the real woman, discover your original voice and tempo, explore your unpainted feelings, find the parts of your personality you despised and suppressed. We have to be open emotionally and spiritually for the Lord to define who we are. It might mean righting past wrongs and letting go, but God never forces us to let something go, but he brings us to a place where we want to give it over for the sake of something far better.

When Shakespeare penned, "All the world's a stage" (*As You Like It*), I wonder if he gave it any spiritual thought. It's exactly the thought I pondered a few weeks ago when I bought a mug with the famous saying scrawled on it along with young men in renaissance costume playing a hand of cards.

> All the world's a stage,
> And all the men and women merely players:
> They have their exits and their entrances;
> And one man [or woman] in his time plays many parts.[4]

If we believe in a sovereign God who directs the affairs of men, then we can't help but see ourselves, created and designed by him, with a written-for-us part to play in his grand story, in his perfect time. I think of Esther, a woman prepared and positioned by God. Hers is a rich and wonderful tale of how God works behind the scenes, casting the roles, placing the people in the right places at the right time to bring about his perfect ending.

It was Oliver Wendell Holmes who said most people go to their graves with the songs still left in them. I don't want to be one of them. I think of an actor who spends months studying her lines but never shows up for the first rehearsal. She stands on the sidelines, waiting for the call; the problem is, the call has already come. The part is hers. Either she failed to recognize the voice or she was just too scared to face the audience.

Though my drama career was short-lived, I managed to observe a few things about good directors. The best ones have been in the performer's shoes and understand what it's like to study and rehearse all their lines and still feel awkward and insecure at the audition. So a good director gives the actor time to be familiar with the role she is about to play, to commit fully to the depth of the character. Good directors help an actor draw on her emotions, dig deep into her soul, and get in touch with the real feelings.

The best director knows his actor, studies her personality, and intuitively knows how to elicit the response he wants in any given scene. And a great director always knows how best to shape the actor for the role she is about to play.

Once a director has the script and has cast the actors, the focus changes. It's all about the story. Won't you let God, the Great Director, begin to shape you for the part?

Digging in Together

1. What roles do you play in your life: mother, sister, colleague, cook, wife, friend, lover, Bible study teacher? Now try to separate yourself from your role. Do you know who you are apart from them?

2. What parts of Jan's story resonate with you?

3. What has been your definition of the abundant life (John 10:10)? How has this belief affected your life so far?

4. How does it encourage you to know that God chips away at our stubborn habits and beliefs? See John 15:1–2. *prunes/cuts*

5. Look at John 17:17–19; 1 Corinthians 6:11; and 1 Thessalonians 5:23–24. How do these verses relate to unmasking?

6. What would you like to gain from this study? How would you like to be different when it's over?

John 17: truth
1 Cor 6:11 Made right w/ God
1 Thes. make you holy

Chapter 2

Backstory

There's always a story behind the story. And God knows it all.

O Lord, you have searched me
and you know me. . . .
You are familiar with all my ways.
(Psalm 139:1, 3)

There's nothing like live theater. Every performance is fresh, something is always slightly different. No two nights are ever the same. Anything can happen. So it is with life. It's the unpredictability that makes it a soul-stirring journey.

I remember sitting in the audience of my first professional stage production, *The King and I,* in San Francisco, entranced by the singing, dancing, props, and costumes. The actors lingered in the lobby afterward—their makeup moist with sweat from the theater lights—to sign the playbills. I thought, what a magical life. I can see myself doing this someday.

Joining the drama club in high school, I auditioned for every school play. In my last year, a friend and I entered the annual, much applauded contest to write our senior class musical. We had no clue about writing scripts, except they are structured in three acts. So Jill and I decided to wing it. There was no Internet in those days to surf for tips, and we never thought to visit the library. We just brainstormed a story—a spoof on Cinderella set in a Wild West town—and created characters from the kids we knew, added some very funny dialogue about life, love, and growing up, and rewrote the lyrics to popular songs.

To Be or Not to Be: She Wasn't won the contest. Never mind there were only three entrants, our script was chosen. Of course, I had written a juicy part for myself—the Annie Oakley-type fairy godmother with an attitude and a six-shooter—but our director didn't see the genius in this and cast someone else.

I landed the role of the wicked scheming stepmother who managed the town saloon, later dubbed a "milk bar" after much deliberation by the school management. How times have changed. I wondered if this casting decision was an indication of what the director really thought of me, but I never had the courage to ask. Maybe at our next class reunion.

Years later, now serious about writing, I enrolled in a screenwriting class, convinced of my incredible talent in this arena. Hollywood was calling. And wouldn't Ron Howard go bananas over my historical romance and offer me an option on it?

Our class assignment was to write backstories of all our characters, the set of significant events that occurred in the character's past that shaped her—where she grew up and went to school, her childhood crises, hopes, dreams, and hang-ups, everything that happened to her before the story starts. "You need to know more about your characters than your audience will," the writing teacher said.

"Backstory" is movie jargon for the history behind the story. It's the third dimension that all characters must have. All well-rounded characters have an existence that lies behind their words and actions.

"Seeing how they were shaped helps you understand why they respond the way they do to the scenes you write," the teacher insisted. "You as the author are in an inseparable and symbiotic relationship with the people you create. You alone hear each distinct voice and know their soul's deepest longings."

What a spiritual connection, I mused. God, as our creator, is the author of our story, and only he has the only true and intimate knowledge of our past. "You know me inside and out. . . . You know exactly how I was made, bit by bit," David wrote in the Psalms, "how I was sculpted from nothing into something. Like an open book, you watched me grow from conception to birth; all the stages of my life were spread out before you. The days of my life all prepared before I'd even lived one day" (Ps. 139:15–16 MSG).

This truth can either bug you or bless you. It all depends on your perspective.

One of the common terms in class was what they call *intentionality* of the character. What does the character want, and want desperately? The story starts here when the main character reaches for her goal and hits a snag. Then another and another. Characters are revealed by the choices they make in the presence of conflict. The more demanding the choice, the more revealing the character.

If you're a writer tackling a script or a novel, you want to create a protagonist who struggles. Have you ever walked out of the theater and asked yourself, "Why did I like this movie or play?" No doubt it's because the main character wasn't cardboard; she grew and evolved—it's called an arc—and she changed in some profound way due to the conflict she faced in the story. One of my most loved stage plays is *Seven Brides for Seven Brothers,* a hootin' and hollerin' musical I can watch repeatedly. Adam, the oldest of seven brothers, goes to town for a wife and charms Milly—who feels hopeless in her situation—into marrying him that same day. When they return to his backwoods home, she finds his six slovenly brothers all living in the cabin, and she's been recruited to clean up after them. Milly sets out to reform the rascals, and it nearly ruins her marriage. In the end, she grows as a woman and a wife, and Adam becomes the man she hoped he would be.

Don't we love stories where the characters grow and emerge with a new outlook on life because of the incredible odds they face? My personal favorites are stories where a character is pursuing one goal but has no idea—but the audience usually does—she is going to end up with something far better.

Of course in a play there is struggle, but it always gets resolved in about two hours.

In my pre-Christian days I related to Dorothy in the *Wizard of Oz* when she yearns to go where there isn't any trouble. "Do you suppose there is such a place?" she asks Toto, and then decides that it must be somewhere over the rainbow.

Where troubles melt like lemon drops . . .

As a child I saw God as the old wizard, choreographing the world from behind a giant curtain while smoke billows out from its folds. Do you remember the scene where Dorothy stands shaking in fear while the wizard belts out, "And what do you want from the Great and Powerful . . . ?"

That was me, minus the ruby red slippers, expecting God to send me to kill the wicked witch. I believed there was a God and prayed now and then, but I never expected an answer nor intimacy of any sort, nor a friendship nor, better yet, a love relationship with him. *I know you're there, somewhere, but you're a bit terrifying for me. Plus if you start talking to me, you might direct me to stay single the rest of my life or go to Africa and be a missionary. No thanks. I like running my own life.*

When I speak at women's events, I always share my backstory, the painful but no longer shameful events that shaped me. The messy stuff in my childhood, a date rape in college and stillborn child, my dream of a white picket fence future shattered by divorce, and prodigal daughters. I choose to be transparent so others will see the value in owning our backstory, in being real about who we are.

Countless women approach me afterward with the same comments. "You lived my life." Or "Your backstory is so much like mine, I can't believe it." I find that many women have mixed messages about themselves and their true worth because their view of God is as distorted as mine once was.

They have difficulty seeing how they fit in God's plan, and they don't yet see that he wants to turn our mess into our ministry.

We often miss the value in our backstory. When I first went to Karen for counseling, I went to fix my daughter and find some options for managing my chaotic life. Intent on staying focused on the present, I was done with the past, or so I thought. Okay, so it was rough and miserable at times and people I trusted betrayed me. So what? I can't go there. I don't have the time or the energy now. Food needs to go on the table.

To her credit, Karen knew to hit me hard with the truth of my coverup.

The more we mask our real self, squash it, bash it, hide it, and hate it, the more we risk a slow death to the essence of who we are.

We're tempted to put too cheap a price on our past. We see it as a waste product of our life and discount its worth. How we miss the mark on that one. Our past is our prize.

The Death of Dreams

Look at Esther. Yes, she rose to become a queen, but little Hadassah (her Hebrew name) did not start out life as a pampered princess. Esther's parents may have been exiles who opted to stay in Persia after the Jews were given their freedom. We don't know this part of her backstory, but we know she faced loss early in life; we're told she was an orphan, raised by her cousin Mordecai. Whenever I see the word *orphan* in the text, it jumps from the page like an anxious toddler from his bed in the morning.

Flipping to the never-too-far-from-my-side thesaurus, I find words like *left behind, abandoned,* and *discarded.* Haven't we all felt this way at crisis times in our lives? And what an accurate sketch of me at the beginning of my Christian walk. Emotionally abandoned by my mother. Discarded by my childhood sweetheart. Even my daughters, in their rebellion, were trying to run out on me.

Stray is another synonym for *orphan* that fits us today. In my travels I meet women who confess they've lost their direction, and many come to a weekend retreat hoping to get their HPS (Heavenly Positioning System) working again. And a few arrive still convinced they are tough and unbreakable, and they tell me how they almost bailed out and went home because my stories hit so close to their hiding place. They stayed, and God broke through.

I love Esther's story in the book named for her. I'm not going to recap it for you—others have done it so much better—but please take time to read it on your own. As in the best of scripts, the story begins with a crisis. The curtain opens on King Xerxes' after-battle banquet for his top commanders. The drunken king summons Queen Vashti to parade in front of his men friends, but she refuses. Whoops. Wrong move because the king's advisors insist he ditch her and find a new queen, or else every other wife will be impossible to live with.

So there's a call-out for a provincial beauty pageant. The fairest maidens—all must be virgins—are drafted for the contest. Wouldn't this make a ratings buster reality show? Esther had no choice but to be part of the royal roundup. Some Bible versions say she was "taken" to the palace, probably against her will. She must now exploit herself like a prostitute for a chance to win a heathen king. There would be no white picket fence future for her. Her dream of marriage to a nice Jewish boy is kaput, over.

Win or lose this contest, she would most likely be the king's property. A queen or a concubine existed solely for the king's sexual pleasure—if he ever summoned you. Life at the royal harem could be a lonely place.

Dreams die even for biblical queens.

So one moment Esther is making plans for her life, and the next she is thrown into a situation that tests everything she trusts. She has no choice; she must go against God's moral law and bed a heathen king. How do you cope with something like that? You can't, unless you know and trust God, unless you have a clear picture of who he is and how nothing he ever does is without a good purpose, no matter how it may appear.

We aren't promised it will be easy, only that we'll have the strength and grace to endure whatever comes.

"I Haven't Got Time for the Pain"

In the year after my fateful counseling visit, this concept went from my head to my heart and insights popped like fireworks throwing light on my dark places. My unmasking was like going to the Fun House, that carnival attraction with distorted mirrors in every misshapen room; there was not one angle from which I liked my reflection.

I had repressed so much of my pain—thirty plus years' worth—and controlled the tears so long, I felt like the Dutch boy with his finger stuck in the hole in the dyke, trying to hold back the flood.

When Jesus said, "Do not let your hearts be troubled," he knew our response would sometimes be, *I am super troubled, Lord, and my well is too deep. Dredging up all this gunk is a messy deal. Can't we leave the past alone? So what if the water is a bit muddy? It won't kill me.*

No, but it will clog up your life over time. Like my friend Mary Lee says often in Sunday school: What's at the bottom of the well comes up in the bucket.

Each week I came to Karen's office to talk—and talk and talk. Travel through reruns of my childhood with the help of a Cabbage Patch doll. This toy rage of the 1980s is making a comeback now. The soft sculptured dolls are not sold but "adopted," and come with official birth certificates.

Let's call mine "Abbey." She had close-set eyes, reddish blond curls, a pudgy face, stumpy arms, and baggy denim overalls. If you saw my toddler pictures you'd know there was a symbolic connection going on here.

"Tell me what you were like as a little girl," Karen said as she handed me Abbey. Holding her I felt the dam ready to burst open and flood the canyon of my soul. "What do you remember about little Jan?" she asked.

I tried to recall something. Just blank spots. Nothing emerged. No memories of a happy toddler prancing through the house crying "Mama." My early memories were blocked; I couldn't find my backstory. Right then I had the overwhelming urge to throw Abbey out the window.

It took a few more sessions but I conjured up an image of school-age Jan thinking, *If only I'm good enough, maybe Mom will love me.*

Bingo—I had just defined the driving force of my entire life: acceptance and approval.

Then it happened, my life unfolded like a Power Point presentation, with God pausing after each scene, and I could sense him speaking to my heart: *Can you see why you made this decision? Can you see how you collected this wrong attitude? Now, can you let it go? Can you forgive that past hurt? No? Then we'll come back around and view it later.*

Uncovering the truth was torture: my addiction to approval, my darkness of self-doubt, my compulsion to fix everybody. In my quest for acceptance, I made compromises, started memorizing a bad script and rehearsing for the wrong role. As I began really hearing myself, it was the voice of a desperate woman who felt like a failure; she couldn't hold her man or control her daughters. I was a flop.

Over time I heard the cries of the little girl lost, reaching out to attach to me again like Peter Pan's shadow. Still, I couldn't dredge up a good cry. I'd done it once for a solid week after my husband walked out, and it was a dismal sight. I was not about to lose control in Karen's office. One day she folded her notebook early and said, "Go home and embrace the pain. Let the God of the universe wrap his arms around you." A strange concept for a gal who knew only how to hide the pain, not hug it. I had no clue what she meant.

On my lips were the words to a song I'd sung in other scenes: Carly Simon's tune, "I Haven't Got Time for the Pain."

But desperation has a way of bringing on surrender. That night, with my daughters asleep, I stoked up a fire in the wood stove. As the oak logs crackled and glowed, I sat on the braided throw rug and wrapped my arms in a big bear hug, rocking back and forth, praying. Suddenly, I gave way to unrecognizable groaning. I beat the carpet with my clenched fists and cried spastic out-of-control tears. Then a strange stillness came upon me, like a hush from heaven.

I had come into the presence of God and sensed him saying, "I'm here in the midst of your pain, Jan. Wrestle with me until all your issues are settled." And so I did, for much of the night, blabbering on like a little girl with a new understanding of what it means to pour out your heart like water in the presence of the Lord (Lam. 2:19). I clearly heard the call, *Return to me, come home to yourself. You've been running, seeking solace in all the wrong places. Stand still and receive it from me.* It was at that moment I understood what closeness with God would mean in my life.

I would still have his love in the morning.

Eureka! I got it! This is what grace really is, the loving look on God's face when he reviews my life, when he coaxes me to come with my genuine tears and unveiled frankness. When we change and follow the Lord, Paul said, our masks—our veils—are taken away: "The Lord is the Spirit, and where the Spirit of the Lord is, there is freedom. Our faces, then, are not covered" (2 Cor. 3:17–18 NCV).

Freedom is one of the first words we hear in our faith beginnings. Our salvation means freedom from sin and death. Okay, we grasp that and it's comforting, but what we really want is some relief from the weariness of life right now, to figure out how to make it work well until we can meet our Maker. Understanding our life is an elusive thing until we know how to gaze on Jesus, with nothing to hide. A steady gaze until our hearts and minds become mirrors that reflect his truth in its proper light.

And then something wonderful will happen: we comprehend with our spirit what our mind already knows, that God is a living, personal presence, and nothing can ever come between us except our own deceptions.

Paul said, "We are being changed to be like him."(2 Cor. 3:18 NCV). That's the simple and complex truth of it.

Jesus never demanded answers from God, but embraced his sorrow. When he cried out, "My God, why have you forsaken me?" (Matt. 27:46), he was expressing the agony in his heart. Like him, we can embrace our sorrow until we feel God's love and can say, "Yes, Lord, I know you're there."

The Power of Pain

I think of what C. S. Lewis said about pain—that it's God's "megaphone to rouse a deaf world."[1] An inattentive and unwilling world that is lost. Pain is always a wake-up call, and if we can only resist that awful urge to torpedo it—sink it out of sight like I did—pain becomes a springboard to spiritual authenticity.[2] We become a woman tuned into the real God, who quits faking it and is willing to be the woman God created her to be.

You may be hurting about something in your life right now, feeling all smashed up by your circumstances; your life is chaotic and messy, and I give you permission to admit that everything is not okay.

It's what I call unmasked honesty, and I believe it's the only way to an authentic relationship with the Lord. Take it from one who's paid the price: unexpressed pain turns to poison, but pain expressed turns to energy—energy to heal, to love, energy for our mission in life, energy to serve God and others in a healthy way.

Look at how the Hebrew people had a handle on grieving. The Psalms are filled with expressions of pain, all penned in the language of brokenness, music to God's ears. The Psalms are a prescription for us, permission to divulge our pain and doubts to the Lord in honest uncamouflaged conversation. At first I saw the Psalms as poems of praise and worship;

then I took a closer look. More than half are songs of lament, full of lots of hand wringing.

They show David in the pit of despair, hiding in a cave, being blunt with his God. *Hey God, are you not paying attention? I'm falling apart down here. My enemies surround me. I need some help. Where are you? Have you abandoned me?*

The Old Testament prophets knew the value of crying out to God. Jeremiah wept, his eyes overflowing with tears (Lam. 1:16), and he calls to us to "pour out your heart[s] like water" (Lam. 2:19). Joel told the Jews how God wanted them to grieve: "Cry loudly like a young woman who is dressed in sackcloth, mourning for the man she was going to marry" (Joel 1:8 *God's Word*) We may not slip into our sackcloth as the Israelites did to declare our sorrow and brokenness, but every woman knows what it means to cry buckets over losing the man she loves.

And sure, we nod our heads when we read James 1:2 and are told to "consider it pure joy" when we face trials, and somehow we believe we'll see the "sheer gift" in it, as *The Message* says, but in the midst of our pain, let's get real about it and feel it to the fullest.

That's the way to freedom.

Our friends and well-wishers might encourage us to "buck up" and move on, find a replacement for what we've lost, but that's the world's way, not God's. He urges us to cry out in our sorrow. "Those who plant in tears will harvest with shouts of joy. They weep as they go to plant their seed, but they sing as they return with the harvest" (Psalm 126:5–6 NLT).

It's vital that you have the right perspective of your backstory. Yes, it's normal when you run up against trouble in life to ask, Why is this happening to me? And it's not strange to entertain the thought that maybe it's a punishment for some past flub-up. *What did I do to deserve this?* Finding my marriage abruptly over without my consent, I pondered all the possible reasons. Maybe it happened because I had sinned, losing my virginity to my fiancé before our marriage. I imagined God saying, "Well now you've done it. I can't bless you."

Caught in this mind-set, I concluded that my first marriage was doomed from the start. A case of faulty thinking on my part—which we'll talk about later—that only perpetuated the shame of my situation.

Could I have prevented my mate's leaving us? No, marriage requires two willing hearts, and his wasn't cooperating. Despite my good intentions, I couldn't tie his heart to the hitching post of home.

We try to wipe out the painful past. We look at our backstory as a musty old basement stacked with useless relics of little value, so let's just board the thing up, padlock the door, and forget it exits. We can ignore it just fine, and then one day something snaps, and we find ourselves in major meltdown for no apparent reason. We have a panic attack and wonder where it came from.

If we don't deal with our dark side, it will deal with us. And the time is never convenient.

Emily* from my adult Sunday school is in the thick of unmasking right now. "The stripping hurts so much," she told me at lunch last week. "I just can't control the tears. I'm sorry I'm so transparent," she says, as if being open and unguarded is a curse.

"You remind me so much of myself years ago," I told her. "But your honesty in our Sunday school class is so refreshing. You may not know it, but by revealing yourself, you're causing others to be more open, to be real about what they're really thinking. God is using you, girlfriend."

Raised with four sisters in a fatherless household, she grew up feeling fat and stupid. After four failed marriages—the constant search for love and affirmation—Emily finally had enough of hiding; she gave up and stopped running from God. "I'm racing around the cul-de-sac and keep coming back to the same place. I've got to stop and face my past and get right for once."

Sarah is a young woman in our couples Bible study, and she's no stranger to her dark side. I admire the way she can speak candidly about it. "I have so much junk in my past I know must be healed. I prayed for God to break me down, and now he's doing it, emptying out the darkness so the light can shine through. It's really hard, and I find myself just wanting to run away to escape to the mall." I laugh because I've been there many times.

Sarah admits she went haywire in her youth and traded it for single motherhood at fifteen, and then she struggled with alcohol. But she is beginning to own her backstory. She's learned that it's part of her. Reject it—ignore and keep it hidden—and you reject a gift from God. What's the gift? The keys that open the doors to authentic self, doors that lead to freedom and grace.

For me, grasping that there is a God who really loves me—with a pure and powerful love that I will never understand—made all the difference in accepting my past and all the sordid scenes within it. And not only did God love me, but he desired a personal relationship with me, all of me—my past, my present, my future.

Digging in Together

1. Compare your current view of God with your childhood view of him. How do your views differ? How are they the same?

2. Can you recall a time when you cried cleansing tears like those of Lamentations 2:19?

3. Do you agree that unmasked honesty is the way to authentic relationship with the Lord? Look at 2 Corinthians 3:12–18.

4. How do you feel about the statement, "If you don't deal with your dark side, it will deal with you"? Have you had personal experience with this?

5. With honesty, share how your backstory affects your life today. If you're trapped by your backstory, what will it take for you to accept and own it?

Chapter 3

The Casting Call

You are destined to play God's leading lady.

It's in Christ that we find out who we are and what we are living for. Long before we first heard of Christ and got our hopes up, he had his eye on us, had designs on us for glorious living. (Ephesians 1:11 MSG)

Every Thursday night I drove home from my counseling sessions over twisty miles of country roads feeling like food for worms.

Come to think of it, that's what I was.

Ten years on twenty rural acres made me familiar with the flora, fauna, and amazing ecosystem of the Sierra Nevada foothills where I live in California. My city upbringing never caused me to contemplate the worm, except as something to describe my former husband after he left me. And it was one of the kinder things I called him in those days.

A worm is the best "composter." Give her some old dirt, discarded kitchen scraps, and manure, and she'll happily consume it.

I use the worm metaphor here to describe my feelings in those early days. It felt like holy worms were eating away the masks, rooting out the sludge—the old dross—so I'd be ready to step into my role as God's leading lady.

A hazy concept, but one I tried to grasp with mustard-seed hope.

"We Live According to What We Believe About Ourselves"

Our church sponsors a program called Life Skills, a branch of Life Skills International, a Christian organization that hosts seminars and classes to help people break the patterns of the past. The director attends our Sunday school class, and one day Sheron said, "We live according to what we believe about ourselves."

So true. We see ourselves through our situations. I thought of the bleeding woman of Mark 5. Jesus was on his way to the home of a young man whose daughter was dying, when he was waylaid by a woman with a gushing problem. Literally, she'd been bleeding for twelve years. She sought out Jesus, hoping that if she just touched his cloak she would be healed. This gal took a huge risk, revealing her sensitive and shameful problem in front of a crowd, but utter desperation is an instant cure for shyness. And Jesus took time to heal her on the spot. He knew her dilemma before she revealed it.

Imagine what those twelve years were like for this gal, even if she never had cramps. Trying to control the mess could consume your entire day. And according to ancient Jewish law, touching this woman made you unclean. Her physical condition was not the worst of her problems, not compared to being a social outcast, emotionally alone, condemned for something over which she had no control.

This poor woman had been through the gamut of doctors only to get worse, and she'd reached her breaking point. But when we come to our last straw, we find the courage to push through our handicaps; we change our tune, alter our MO.

That's what my friend Debbie did. Let me give you some of her backstory. In rebellion against what she considered intolerant parents with unusually high standards, she escaped into a teenage marriage. By the time I met up with her about sixteen years ago, she was barely past thirty, divorced twice with children from each union. She had come to our singles fellowship, where God placed me for a season as one of the group leaders.

She had three growing youngsters and not a dime in child support. "I really know how to pick 'em, don't I, Jan?" she quipped one night, poking fun at herself. Underneath, I sensed heart-burning regret that comes with the impulsive choices we make. Debbie worked nights as a receptionist in the emergency room at our community hospital.

Though she enthusiastically agreed with our group's goal of becoming the right person first, she kept secretly thinking, *surely, a man would make it easier.* Oh, what tangled webs we weave when Satan tempts us to self-deceive.

Been there, done that, and have the qualifying T-shirt.

When her oldest son proved more than she could handle, Debbie turned a blind eye to her nagging doubts and sent him to live with his father, convincing herself it was for everyone's good.

How she managed to attend college full time and earn a master's degree in social work is beyond me. They were long hard years of little sleep, no money, thrift store shopping, a junk car, and care packages from her family. Yet Debbie never dropped the "happy face" mask. After our singles fellowship came to its natural end, I saw her only on occasion. She popped into church once in a while, but avoided consistent fellowship. She did check in sometimes to share her latest self-discoveries with the Bible study girls who met at my house.

"I was a recovery program junkie during those days," she says.

When we spoke recently about the topic of this book, she told me, "I was able to obtain my education and other behavior goals, no problem, but never a close relationship with the Lord."

It kept eluding her. Or rather, she maintained a respectable and safe distance from him.

Years went by, and we lost touch. After a decade of singleness I met Carl, and two years later we married. Debbie came to our wedding at an old Victorian house to celebrate God's goodness with us, but we lost touch for a while as I adjusted to couple-hood and she built a career as a medical social worker. Then one day an invitation arrived for a wedding in Lake Tahoe. *Debbie and her second ex-husband are remarrying? What? The guy with alcohol problems; the one who's bipolar with a history of extramarital affairs?*

I grabbed the phone and called to get the scoop.

"It just seems so natural to get married," she said, "since he's been renting a room from me for a year. He's been on probation, you know for that fraud conviction."

Gulp. Somehow that fact had escaped me. The social worker in Debbie had stepped forward to rescue this needy man. "We are so used to each other now. I guess it's a relationship of convenience."

Yikes. It's come to this? In the past decade I'd seen Debbie's weight soar as her confidence plunged like a skydiver whose parachute didn't open. I knew Debbie well enough to hear what her words weren't saying. *Maybe this marriage is the answer to my loneliness. After all, men are not exactly beating down the door these days, the way I look.*

In my heart I heard the foghorn—treacherous waters dead ahead—but Debbie's mind was set, the wedding was on, so I sent my RSVP.

The union lasted through two years of inconsistency and infidelity. When she called me with the news that it was over, she announced it with calloused relief, "It was a mistake. I'm glad to be done with it." No tears, no regret. Debbie wore the mask of indifference. Just toss this backstory in the Basement of Boo-boos and pretend the marriage never really happened.

Many months passed and one morning waiting in line at LaBou for my favorite coffee, I saw Debbie. Rather she saw me—I never recognized her until she tapped me on the shoulder. "Jan, it's Debbie."

Huh? What? This wisp of a woman is Debbie? She was half of her former self. She looked so different, and so good. "I had gastro-bypass surgery," she whispered. "I've lost a hundred-plus pounds."

And a lot more excess baggage I soon found out after she left a message on my machine that she had "something very important to share with me."

Oh, oh. My first thought—not another bridal march. I'll be out of town.

When we finally connected, she said, "Jan, my life has been such a mess, and I refused to confront it. After the divorce, I threw myself into work to advance my career. I took advantage of this amazing surgery, and as I got lighter in body I only got heavier in spirit."

Isn't that the way? Why do we think that by beautifying our body we'll be beautifying our life?

"And then I severely hurt my back and neck and had to stop working and go on disability," she added. As the months wore on, she had nothing but time to think and ponder. "I was in so much pain, but dealing with the physical pain was not the battle; it was with the condition of my spirit. I found myself constantly wrestling with God, and it hurt so bad. I felt so alone and disconnected."

Accepting Our Role as God's Leading Lady

Then Debbie came to the place of the bleeding woman, desperate for a healing touch from Jesus. "I finally fell on my knees and said, 'Lord, I can't take it anymore. I'm miserable. I can't work, and I can't survive on disability. Help me.' And you know what he seemed to say to me? Debbie, do you want to go around that same mountain one more time? You know what to do. Drop the masks and get real with me."

She'd been attending a church near her house for a few months. "On a whim, I joined the women's Bible study on God's promises at Celebration Church. What an eye-opener for me. Sure, we all know about God's promises—the Bible is full of them—but I never realized until going through this study that God meant them for me. Me, Debbie, the three time loser.

"The truth—Jan, I've never gotten the joy, peace, and victory in my life as a Christian, and I've always wondered why. Not until now did I face the truth. I blamed God for all of my problems; if he loved me he'd have kept me from blowing it so badly. Rescued me from myself. I blamed him and my parents for the stupid decisions I ultimately made."

Hiding behind the mask of the successful professional did the trick until she was injured on the job and trapped at home, told to stay quiet and rest her body. "And I had no choice. I couldn't escape the Lord by keeping busy. He was there, calling me to look in the mirror and see myself as I really am, stripped of all pretenses. It cut like a knife, and I spent days and days just sobbing, but that's what it took for me to finally surrender.

"I could finally tell God: 'I don't want what Debbie wants anymore. I'm tired of living Debbie's way. Debbie is so stubborn. I want to be the woman you want me to be.'"

Though she had no idea how she'd manage to pay the bills, she kept sensing from God, "Try something new. Try trusting me, Debbie, and see how I'll meet all your needs."

A defining moment for this leading lady. "God immediately started chipping away at the areas that prevented me from being the type of woman he would have me to be, removing the mask of pride, teaching me about humility, mercy, grace, and forgiveness. I think he was just waiting for me to get to a point where I could admit my honest need for him. And, Jan, what a revelation—he is worth trusting. Everyone else, including the men in my life, always ended up abandoning me. But our God is reliable."

So true. As the Lord lifts our masks we get the first real unvarnished glimpse of ourselves, and it's always awkward. It's like trusting yourself with the specialist after you've been scarred in an accident and need reconstructive surgery. You don't know for sure that the promises he made for your new face will come to pass, but you have no choice. You either trust him for a makeover, or you stay scarred. So you go under the knife or the laser. You want healing so much that you're willing to risk it.

Then comes the final unwrapping. You've probably seen this in a movie—I saw one not too long ago—where the doctor removes the bandages and the patient finally sees what she looks like. She shrinks back in shock at first, surprised at how different she is. It takes a while for her eyes to accept her new look.

Although raised in an evangelical church all her life, Debbie admits that her walk with the Lord was never real. "In our church everything was a sin, and you came to repent and recommit every Sunday. I learned to just fake it, to draw on my innate skill at playing charades. My faith looked real on the surface. Nobody knew. I got good at polishing up my exterior, and it became a way of life."

Something her now-adult son needed to hear from his mother. "I needed to give him honesty, no more of the religious jargon I fed him for years," she said. "And I lived with so much guilt over letting him go, so I let him know this and asked his forgiveness. How freeing that was; what walls came down for both of us."

Debbie is coming to understand and accept her backstory, the truth of the way she craved favor and affection from people—and men—but never from God.

In the midst of all this, Debbie's first ex-husband (the one she only married once) showed up at the door, needing to talk. "He told me it's time to get his life straightened out and come clean with everything that's hanging over his past. And that includes paying the back child support he owes me," Debbie related. "I almost fell over. I had let go of ever seeing a dime of it."

As it turns out, a substantial windfall had come his way, and after some soul searching he decided to square up with Debbie. "So there we were in my living room talking, for the first time ever, about our teen-age marriage and why it failed. I found myself asking his forgiveness for some of the choices I made, choices that I knew contributed to his leaving and abandoning the family."

Debbie admits she refused to accept an ounce of responsibility for anything, dumping it on everyone else instead—parents, ex-husbands, even God.

According to the district attorney's office, which tried unsuccessfully to collect her back child support, her first husband owed her a whopping $69,000 including interest. Debbie's first response was to say, "That's too much. I'll just take the original amount he owes me and forgive all the interest that accrued over the years."

Confused, she went to her pastor for counsel. "What makes you feel you don't deserve the full amount?" Pastor Cedric inquired.

At the word *deserve* Debbie felt herself cower inside. "I guess it goes back to my value as a child," she told me. "My tendency to take less than God's best in almost every area of my life. The belief that I was destined to accept second fiddle . . . something that has carried into my adulthood."

Her pastor encouraged her to accept all the money owed her, guilt free. "He needs to do the right thing, and you need to let him. This is how God is working to grow him. The reward works both ways."

An angle she hadn't considered.

"Oh, Jan, talk about restoring the years the locusts have eaten," Debbie said. "It's amazing. Just at my time of need, God stands true to his word. And I know it's happening now at this time because for the first time in my forty-nine years I chose to dump the disguise. I want to get real with him and show others what it's like to live in right relationship. I'm in awe of how much he loves me, despite how much I betrayed him, how he's touched me and is teaching me how to forgive and truly love myself. If I would have known how good it would be—an authentic relationship with him—I would have surrendered long ago, but it doesn't work that way, does it? We need to go through the refining fire. It makes the reward—the intimate fellowship—much more precious."

Debbie is ready now to accept her role as God's leading lady. It means believing about ourselves what God does—that we are of great value to him. We have to settle the issue of his love and faithfulness. Debbie's view of God is a common one—Big Daddy in the Sky, mysterious and angry, accusing her of not measuring up. How do you relate to a God like that? Debbie couldn't. But she finally discovered that she is his chosen child, and he wants to love her. Then the light of truth switched on.

As we ended our conversation that afternoon, Debbie said, "Jan, I've avoided you the last few years."

"Why?"

"You were one of the leaders of our singles group, so grounded in your faith; you always urged us to stick to the hard line and do the right thing. How could I let you know what was really going on in my life? I wanted you to be proud of me."

Wow. During my whirl as a singles leader, I saw it as my duty to be a moral compass, but in an honest look back, it was a mask that kept people from being real with me. *Oh, Debbie, thank you for your unvarnished honesty. What a gift.*

Debbie finally fired herself as the star of her one-woman show. Her performance was flat and the applause empty. When she requested her name be removed from the flashing neon marquis, an amazing thing occurred. God turned the spotlight back on her, and she's now glowing with a light she never had before.

Winston Churchill, the famous British politician, once said, "We are all worms at one time or another, but I do believe I am a glowworm."[1]

That's what I call true star power.

Digging in Together

1. How true is the statement "We live according to what we believe about ourselves"? Give examples of this truth in action.

2. If, like the bleeding woman, you met Jesus on the road, what would you ask him to heal right now?

3. Has there ever been a time in your life when God used a physical condition to help you gain spiritual growth and insight? Share your story with the group.

4. In what ways do Christians fake their faith? Why are we prone to polish up our exterior for other Christians?

5. Like Debbie, have you sought approval from people and not from God? How can Paul's words found in Galatians 1:10 encourage us in this area of life?

Obviously, I'm not trying to win approval of people, but of God. If pleasing people were my goal, I would not be Christ's servant.

Intermission

It's humming with activity behind the curtain. The wardrobe lady adds the final touches to the costumes for the next act—a broad-brimmed straw hat for the heroine, a shiny black cloak for the villain—as the prop master orders the stagehands to switch out the furniture and change the décor.

Props are essential to every show. They serve as a support for the characters and the storyline. What's a play without them? If you've ever sat in a dark theater watching a play, you know it's the props, the painted backdrop of a city skyline or rambling old barn, the plywood pine trees, or the fake spiral staircase, that add interest and color to the production.

Actors need the right props, around which they block their scenes, and props help them know where to stand when delivering their lines. Each prop has a designated time to appear and a distinct position.

But props out of place can mean a major slipup.

Act 2

Glitches

Act 2 is an act of complications. Despite our leading lady's desire to unmask and show her real and most beautiful face to the world, her disguises have grown too familiar. Old defenses, stubborn habits, and pet beliefs are like an old bathrobe, comfortable and hard to throw away. Her past ways of coping clash with her present longing for the full and abundant life.

She underestimated the glitches that hinder her progress, especially being heckled by the enemy, "It's too hard, give it up." Every scene presents some new conflict as she takes an honest look at herself in light of the truth of God. And complications pile up like messy laundry. The audience is on the edge of its seats wondering what will happen to our heroine now. Will she be sabotaged by her own frustration?

Jesus said in Matthew 9:17: "No one puts new wine into old wineskins" (NLT). She's being transformed, renewed—the supreme spiritual makeover—and it means trading her counterfeit self for the real one, her strength for the Spirit's, learning new ways to live and love herself, others, and God. In act 2, we see our leading lady feel the pressure to change and grow.

Yes, she wants it, but it's a difficult journey. And the defining and dramatic question is always this: are you willing to let go and trust that God's plans are good, though you may not understand his methods?

Chapter 4

Competing for the Role

In the compare and compete game nobody is a winner.

Everyone who competes in the games goes into strict training. They do it to get a crown that will not last; but we do it to get a crown that will last forever. (1 Corinthians 9:25)

In my first role as wage earner—breadwinner and single mom—I found myself employed by the California State Legislature at the Capitol in Sacramento. A bizarre turn of events for me, considering my lack of college degree, but I fudged a bit on my resume to make myself more employable and faked an interest in politics. Plus I could scorch the keyboard and write dynamite letters, so I was hired by a senator's office to answer constituent mail. "What is the senator's stand on water rights?" "Is the logging industry dead in the north state?" "What's this I hear about a bill to ban wood burning stoves?"

Penning letters—later speeches—in the voice of a public official proved a stretch even for me, the great pretender. But I got quite good at it, and, never fear, the senator always approved each letter and put his personal signature to it. Staffers don't have *that* much power.

Whenever the subject of higher education came up, I bluffed my way through the conversation; my only university experience was a course on raising dairy goats I took through the University of California at

Davis extension program. My master's program was a class from the county agriculture commission.

At work I struggled with the comparison game. I looked at all the talented, sharp women working in "the building," as we called it, helping draft legislation and steer it through the committee process, negotiating with lobbyists, and addressing interest groups when they stormed the Capitol demanding action. I lumbered with my insecurities while other women seemed to grasp the important issues.

You see, I'd spent my last decade on a country ranch grasping the art of raising livestock. What good was that?

Outside work, I questioned my mothering ability. My number one daughter Jennifer, wearing her mask of tough girl, decided to move away from my supervision, insisting she could support herself and finish high school. She had worn me out so much by that time that I stopped fighting with her. Her younger sister, Amy, was well on her way to prodigal land—smoking, skipping school, dabbling in drugs and bad boyfriends.

I was trapped on a runaway roller coaster, gripping the rails in fervent prayer that God would keep it from derailing.

Other single moms were raising kids in broken homes, and their offspring weren't acting out like my girls. Okay, I told myself, our family scenario is unique because my girls' dad resigned his role as a father, abandoning them to start a new family. This broke my heart, and I still can't imagine that kind of pain for a daughter. My girls' response *must* be normal, right? Not much consolation. I still wondered, *what's the matter with me and why can't I fix this?*

The Comparison Game

Maybe you can relate to playing the comparison game. It begins in childhood when we start sizing ourselves up against our siblings—in my case the neighbor girls—and measure who's the prettiest, smartest, most popular, talented, or the favored child. That one might hit closer to home. Our street was home to fourteen girls in the same age range, all competing for top billing. One summer we put on the play *Little Women* in my garage with my clever script—twelve-year-old style—an adaptation of my favorite book. I saw myself as Jo March, the spirited tomboy who dreams of being a writer.

Oh, did the prima donnas show up for this one, sparring over who would get the plum role. As an only child I was untutored in the art of sisterly spats, so I backed out of the competition. With my best plastic smile I agreed to play Meg, the nice—but boring—sister and congratulated my neighbor pal who manipulated her way into the part of Jo. When she sets her cap for something, she gets it, I thought. Why can't I have that kind of moxie?

Because I like to keep the peace, that's why. And I don't like anyone to be mad at me.

Resentment boiled, bitterness began to breed like mosquitoes in a murky pond when I added up her plusses and compared them to mine. But we stayed best friends for years anyway.

"When we play the comparison game," says Brenda Waggoner, author of *The Velveteen Woman,* "we see ourselves as either better or worse than the other person. Whether we end up on top or on bottom, it's a lose-lose deal."[1]

Take Rachel in Genesis 30, consumed with jealousy for her sister Leah who blessed Jacob with sons when Rachel could not. She tells Jacob, "Give me children or I'll die!" In those days childlessness meant disgrace for a woman. Ancient customs allowed men several wives, and one without babies feared rejection from her husband. Rachel's envy kept her caught in her schemes to one-up Leah. She just didn't get it, Jacob loved her—he'd waited seven years for her—and her infertility didn't matter.

Isn't it funny how we seldom compare ourselves to someone in worse shape than us, except to give our egos a stroke. Then pride rears its ugly head big time. We usually fix our gaze on someone more successful, and we scowl and kick ourselves. We look at *her* and she seems to attract success, and we're scraping by. Besides that, *she* can eat thick crust pan pizza every night and never gain an ounce while we plump up on the skinny crust with fat free cheese.

We heave a wistful sigh at life's unfairness.

The comparison game is laced with traps and we whine, "It's not fair God." Translated to mean, "You don't know what you're doing in my life." There's no freedom in this, just the opposite.

Then why do we zero in on a more attractive woman with more

spendable income, a more sparkling personality, a better marriage, and a handier husband, whose kids are performing better in school and whose teenagers toe the line, at least when Mom is watching. Aiming our sights on *her* makes us feel like a soggy newspaper in the driveway on a rainy morning.

Our sane minds know that God doesn't grade us on our curb appeal—how we look and perform—but we still struggle, it's in our nature. I love what God told Samuel during the search for a new king, "Looks aren't everything. Don't be impressed with his looks and stature. I've already eliminated him. God judges persons differently than humans do. Men and women look at the face; God looks into the heart." (1 Sam. 16:7 MSG)

In other words, image is not where it's at. We don't know what's behind our neighbor's spruced up facade, what painful secrets lurk behind her front door, or what storms are brewing in her heart that she's scared to share for all the same reasons we are. Stop comparing.

During my dozen years at the legislature, God stretched me beyond my imagination. From the first morning I drove to my assigned parking lot on Fifteenth Street to that last afternoon when I turned in my keys and passes, I had changed from an unsure and unstable woman to one with a clearer understanding of the purposes of God for my life.

Still in awe of some of my colleagues' political knowledge and skill, it ceased to matter that mine was in shorter supply. My political handicaps had an upside: they forced me to pay attention—not my strong suit—and pore over research papers and transcripts and hang on the words of lawmakers as they debated the issues. My job was to translate this into the common man's language.

By the time I married Carl in 1995, I made a good salary with nice benefits, but it was a high paced job, and the stress and deadlines wore me out. I had no time for my creative passion, no energy left to write; my frustration ballooned. "Follow your dream, honey," Carl would say. "Quit the job. Life is too short."

Yes, and the cash will be too, I thought. Prior to our wedding, Carl left the corporate world to start a small business, enjoying the freedom it offered, especially time he was able to devote to being an elder of our growing church. But his business receipts barely covered expenses. We needed my income. For a year I hemmed and hawed. Is it irresponsible to leave such a secure job at this stage? *Lord, is this of you? I'm not sure.* The inner nagging would not go away. Then my daughter Jennifer, now married with two small boys, was in a tragic car accident and landed in the hospital with a severe brain injury.

There was my answer. The family needed me now for an extended time. I gave my notice.

Talk about a defining moment. The Lord prepared me by the restlessness in my heart. Without a shove out the door, I may have opted for security and the logical thing, but God's ways are not our ways, and his thoughts not our thoughts (Isa. 55:8).

After cleaning out my desk on my last day in the building, I wandered through the grand renaissance revival building that had been my workplace for more than a decade. I paused at the rotunda where statues of Queen Isabella and Columbus in Italian marble greet visitors from across the state and around the world. I stopped by the senate chamber draped in regal red, the place I often scooted in to deliver important messages to my senator, and I peeked into the committee room on the third floor where they held the weekly Bible study for Capitol staffers.

A silent whimper with every step.

You Are the Message

After three months of recovery in a rehabilitation hospital, Jennifer came home with a positive prognosis. Suddenly, I sat alone at my desk in front of my computer, no strategy sessions to attend or meetings with constituents, no taking school groups on VIP tours of the Capitol. Nobody asking for opinion pieces, policy letters, or speech points. At home I was just a greenhorn writer searching for an assignment. And not one publisher called to say, "We heard you're free to write for us now, and we want you."

As manuscripts went out in the mail, doubts and insecurities rushed in. I felt like Moses after crossing the Red Sea, looking back at Egypt. Back *there* lay the seat of power where once I held a position and had a title and a laminated badge with my photo on it. Back *there* was the place that pulsed with action, where dignitaries came to see the governor, where national headlines were made, where movie stars came to make pitches on their pet causes.

At least I left with some celebrity autographs.

I'd left my identity *back there.* My Red Sea had closed up. There was no turning back.

Without warning, I groped for a new sense of self-worth in the wilderness, wondering if I'd ever reach the Promised Land of publishing. I didn't have forty years to wander, either, unless God intended me to live as long as Moses. I wondered, what kind of fool are you to give up a job like that? *You crazy woman, call your job and see if you can go back now.*

"Give it a year," Carl urged. "Give your all for twelve months and see what happens." *Okay,* so I registered for writers' conferences, and there I met bona fide authors, published writers doing what I longed to do. And what did I do right away? Compare myself to them and let the enemy heckle me with statistics on how many manuscripts never make it past the slush pile, and how most writers never get published. *And you got a late start, girl.*

Shame on you, Jan. You know better than to give the Devil a foothold that way. Resist him and he will flee from you (James 4:7). Most of us give up on our dreams too soon, with the first few rejections. And I had my fill of *We are sorry, but this does not meet our editorial needs at this time.*

Doors slammed shut on my fiction. Then one day I took a workshop teacher's advice: write what you know. I wrote a story of Jennifer's accident, not about the miraculous rescue story, but about finding my faith on the line. Did I really believe Romans 8:28, that all things work together for good? This story, born from a crisis, became my first published Christian work, and it happened within the first year I struck out on my own. My first book wasn't the novel I had planned, but a book rising from the ashes of my ruined dreams, based on my life Scripture, encouraging women to trust in a God who restores.

Maybe I won't give up after all.

After the book was published—and radio interviews told my story—requests arrived to come and speak to women's groups. "Of course, I'd love to," I chirped. Isn't talking one of my gifts? Oh, wouldn't this impress my grammar school teachers who always wrote, "Janis has what it takes to be a good student, but she talks too much in class."

I'd spent years studying speakers, their stage movements, the way they made eye contact, the types of messages shared, the delivery, how they presented their testimonies, and what made the audience laugh or cry. My office files brimmed with audio tapes of speakers I admired. "If only I could speak just like her," I lamented. "If only I could pull truth out of the Bible like she does—motivate, inspire, and turn hearts to Jesus."

And look like she does in the tailored suit. So I went to speaker training for a long weekend to get some tips.

Planning for my first weekend retreat as the guest speaker sent me into a panic; it took two weeks to prepare the four messages, with my notes strewn across my home office floor like a patchwork paper carpet. I tried outlining, laboring over every illustration and scriptural principle. Writing out my script filled with Scriptures I prayed, "Lord, help me be deep and insightful, to share profound and uplifting truths that change lives."

My motives were so genuine, but my presentation was not. I didn't know it then, but I'd fallen back on my masks and disguises and patterned myself after my ideal of what a speaker should be, polished with a flawless presentation.

But like Sonny sang to Cher, "No, no, no, it ain't me babe."

"It's too hard," I whined one Sunday afternoon as Carl unloaded books and props from my car. "It just didn't flow. I'm not cut out for this."

"Get a good night's sleep, honey, and we'll unscramble this tomorrow."

But God beat us to it. During my morning devotional time with *My Utmost for His Highest,* the answer came in the devotional titled "Being an Example of His Message."[2] We are to be instruments of God, he said, not spiritual agents but spiritual messengers and our message must be part of who we are. I looked up *agents* in my trusty thesaurus and words came up like *player, actor, performer.*

Whoops. I had been performing again, and this was God's reminder to unmask and be my authentic self, and deliver *his* message in my own style.

When Chambers tells us to be God's messengers in the flesh, it means allowing God to "set [our] words on fire." Our words, not carefully rehearsed words copying somebody else's style. He gives us words that reflect the way we are uniquely wired.

I made a note in the margin of the devotional: "How profound!" Jesus told stories, simple stories, and turned ordinary situations into powerful object lessons, and eyes were opened, hearts were changed. Here's my journal entry for that day. "*You are the message, Jan. Just be yourself, and tell your stories, from your experiences, in your own way, with your personality. Share the truth about God as it's become real in your life. You have a style all your own. Your playfulness, your wit, the way you communicate biblical truth. It's unique. You're one of a kind. You were born an original. Why do you want to go through life being a copy?*"

That set me free. I come to the platform as me now. I still sometimes forget my glasses and some sweet angel in the front row always offers me hers. I spill my water bottle with my flailing hands and say something unplanned and outrageous, and women come up and thank me for being so natural. Thanks to all of you for affirming that I'm right where I'm supposed to be.

Shouldn't this be our target? To be genuine, authentic, the real deal, and put comparison behind us.

I think of Esther again, living with other virgins in the Royal Harem prepping for her one night with the king. She is now pitted against her roommates in a powerful contest, rivals for the same crown, and only one can win. Wouldn't it bring out the cutthroat in all of us? These girls had one chance to knock the king's crown off. Think of it, girls who might otherwise be your friends are now your competition. Another reality show—Survival of the Sexiest.

By law they must spend twelve months in the beauty parlor; a year of treatments with oils and perfumes, and special foods. They are given servants to see to their every whim: massages, manicures, pedicures, a new hairstyle maybe—I'd press for a thigh reduction myself—anything to enhance their facade. How far are they willing to go to win the king? How far would you go? I, in my weaker moments, would think something like this: *I didn't choose this, but I might as well give it my best shot. I'm stuck here now, and being a queen is better than just a concubine, so desperate measures are necessary. I'd better pull out all the stops. Forget making friends, nobody is going to give me a break. I'm on my own.*

I have to think this was not Esther's attitude. The Bible says she won the favor of everyone who saw her (2:15), and I'll bet it was her pleasing personality. She also made big points with Hegai, the eunuch in charge of the girls, who moved her into the best place in the harem. Wouldn't that raise a few eyebrows? Every smart gal knows that when you're thrown together with other women in fierce competition for only one prize, it can get a bit testy.

I believe Esther made peace with her God in those twelve months, and settled the important issues; life as she knew it would never be the same, and she didn't know why, and may never. When her world fell apart, I'm sure she cried and questioned God, like we all do, then dried the tears and came back to the truth of what she knew, that she was of great value to God and nothing happens to us without purpose. Whether she won or lost the contest, her God would prove faithful. He had a plan, and she had a part in it.

What a perspective. It makes all the difference in how we see life and relate to the other women in our world.

Not in competition but in cooperation. This pleases God and makes him smile. And when it came her time to meet the king, Esther attracted him more than the others. Scripture says she found grace and favor in his sight, and he put the royal crown upon her head (Esther 2:17).

Was it her sensuality that snared the king? Doubtless Xerxes had a choice of a new bed partner every night, the best of the best, but even good sex gets stale and empty when the connection is merely physical. Somehow Esther stood out from the others. Perhaps it wasn't just her beauty and physical charm that made her unique. She alone worshiped the one true God; the Persian women worshiped pagan idols. Their focus remained on the outer covering, they had little control of anything else. But Esther had an inner confidence that came from knowing a personal God and trusting that he was always backstage and knew what was going on up front.

I believe her genuineness dazzled the king, though he hardly knew it at the time.

Can't you see the runner ups comparing notes afterward and sneering: *What does she have that I don't?* Have you been here in your secret thoughts? Me too, and it always moves me away from my girlfriends, not closer to them. In an old movie, buxom film star Mae West says in her throaty voice: "Be the kind of gal who picks her friends . . . but not to pieces."

Last year, an author friend e-mailed me, excited that her new book was "flying off the shelves." My reply was "That's so fantastic, happy for you," but inwardly I whimpered. *What does she have that I don't have? Why do her books sell like crazy and mine don't?*

Just invite a plague of discontent why don't we, Jan? I pinched myself hard. *You're doing it again. You are not in competition with her, don't you get it? You have your purpose, she has hers. Turn your attention to doing what you can and leave the results up to God. Quit counting sales, and start counting souls.*

Doesn't it help to give ourselves a good talking to sometimes?

Galatians tells us, "Make a careful exploration of who you are and the work you have been given, and then sink yourself into that. Don't be impressed with yourself. Don't compare yourself with others. Each of you must take responsibility for doing the creative best you can with your own life." (6:4–5 MSG)

The comparison game, and its spin-off, the competition contest, has been a recurring theme in my life for two years. *You've got to let this go, Jan,* I'd vow. And then wonder YBH. *Yeah, but how?* Then it came to me. *You say you believe that the Lord directs our steps, then live like it, girl.*

Live like it, girl. Live what you believe. If God is your Director on the stage of life, then the part you play is up to him. If someone else gets a better role, it's because he allowed it for a reason. So rejoice for her and taste the freedom in it.

Digging in Together

1. As an adolescent, did you compare yourself to a sibling or school friend? What did she have that you wanted, and did it strain your relationship at all?
2. Who do you play the comparison game with now? Other women,

wives, mothers, coworkers? Share a time when you found your-self in fierce competition for something you both wanted. How did it turn out?

3.   Have you ever felt like Jan after leaving her legislative job, that you lost your identity, that it was back on the other side of the Red Sea? How long did it take to feel confident in your new role?

4.   Read Galatians 5:14–16 and then 5:24–26. Talk about practical ways to find freedom from the comparison game.

Chapter 5

Classical Tragedy

Don't hide in shame and regret. Let the Lord shine his light through it.

There is now no condemnation for those who are in Christ Jesus. (Romans 8:1)

In the months following scene 1 of my marriage rejection story, I threatened to join SCUM, the Society for Cutting Up Men. You should have heard me crooning a litany of the "You Done Me Wrong" songs. Recently, the country music television channel aired a show counting down the top forty "You Done Me Wrong" songs. The all-time favorite: "Your Cheating Heart" . . . and I can recite all the words to that one.

A few of my top picks actually made it on the list: "If You're Gonna Do Me Wrong, Do It Right," and "Whose Bed Have Your Boots Been Under?"

In hindsight it's now funny, because—and jot this one down—comedy is tragedy plus time and a godly perspective.

But back in those days, I had the remote control in my hand reviewing my soap opera life and pausing at the most vivid scenes, especially those with my daughters. I was haunted by the years we missed and was caught between blaming their father and blaming myself. I had chased a relationship while they floundered. I had regrets for them and their lost childhood. If only I could have a second chance, to cuddle with them and share our pain. But overnight my girls weren't little anymore. Why had I let precious time slip away unnoticed?

"It Might Have Been"

John Greenleaf Whittier said, "For of all sad words of tongue or pen, the saddest are these: *it might have been!*"[1]

Regretting our ruined dreams—lost opportunities—can keep us trapped, suspended in a time warp. Over and over I had to loosen my grip on my daughters. From the time Jenny started slipping out her bedroom window to meet her boyfriend, I was consumed with trying to control her. As Amy spiraled into teenage rebellion, so did my obsession with the certainty that she was ruining her life. It tore me apart. I wallowed in a mother's muddled dreams and the heavy cloud of ugly thoughts about both girls' futures.

Letting go of this didn't mean giving up being a concerned parent, but releasing my fears and my daughters to God. He would draw them to himself and heal their wounded hearts in his time. He is the God of restoration, I knew that by now. I couldn't patch up my girls, but he could. My regrets had no positive contribution to my spiritual makeover. Instead they were like depth charges dropping on a submerged submarine.

Sooner or later they would sink me.

The Devil likes it when we relive our battles, wring our hands over our defeats, and lament over what might have been. We linger on thoughts like, "Why was I born into this family?" and "If only I hadn't married this difficult man." He'll remind you constantly of your mistakes until it's hard to discern where his voice stops and yours begins. It's helpful to heed the words of Paul when he said, "Who cut in on you and kept you from obeying the truth? That kind of persuasion does not come from the one who calls you" (Gal. 5:7–8).

I have these wise words from Isaiah highlighted in my Bible, "Forget the former things; do not dwell on the past. See, I am doing a new thing! Now it springs up; do you not perceive it?" (43:18–19). How can we ever spot the divine signposts ahead when we keep wishing we'd taken the last exit? Erasing regret from your life may be one of the biggest obstacles for your spiritual makeover.

Now, there is a time and place for regret, when we can look at it with an honest eye and it becomes a new insight, when it spurs us into action so we change direction. This is not the self-reproach regret, the open-the-old-wounds type of regret, but the *on-second-thought* kind that says, "In retrospect, I'd play this scene a different way."

Off the Record: The Backdrop of Our Secret Shame

There's a rhythm and tempo to life that Solomon best describes in Ecclesiastes: "A time to keep and a time to throw away . . . a time to be silent and a time to speak" (Eccl. 3:6–7).

After reading my book *After the Locusts,* Holly* sent me this e-mail: "I couldn't bring myself to go to sleep tonight without writing to you. After reading your story of the stillborn birth, I burst into uncontrollable sobs, and let out the years of shame, regret and disgust with myself. You see, your first child and mine were born under almost identical circumstances. I have never shared this story with anyone outside my immediate family, but God won't let me sleep until I share it with you."

Like me, Holly was nineteen and away at college when she was betrayed by a man she trusted, who took advantage of her innocence and forced himself on her. Like me, she became pregnant. "I was devastated, ashamed, alone, and too terrified to tell anyone."

We both gave birth to premature stillborn babies, buried our secret, and shored up our lives the best we could.

Fourteen years went by for Holly, fourteen years of masking the pain of her past until she stumbled on my book. "Our stories are so similar. I know that we are soul sisters in a way I've never experienced before. To God be the glory for allowing me to see, through you, that I was never truly as alone as I felt I was before reading your book. I have cried so many tears reading the story we share . . . tears of shame, regret, secrecy, grief.

"Thank you for having the courage to share your painful story and finally giving me the courage to share mine outside my little circle of privacy."

Courage to share this secret didn't come easy. I had thought it was past, done, finished, settled in my heart with God long ago. What's the use of having my daughters—or anyone—aware of this awkward truth, I had wondered. It's better to leave it safely entombed. However, when we bury secrets alive, they never decompose. They accumulate and build up pressure that finally bursts.

Remember me saying that if we don't deal with our dark side, it will deal with us? From the sixth grade on, at least twice a month, I'd be disabled for three days with a throbbing headache that took me to a dark room with an ice pack. Migraines are caused by a tightening of the blood vessels in the head, an abnormal release of neurochemicals in the brain. Those of us with a hypersensitive nervous system are prone to the headaches anyway, but emotional triggers like stress can provoke an attack. And this is also the body's way of releasing the trapped pressure.

Funny how my headaches stopped when I found the guts to face my pain and spill my bag of rotten beans.

When I wrote the book proposal for *After the Locusts,* the outline made no mention of the incidents leading to my first child being stillborn. But I felt a pressure to add it in, and it came on in force. *Why Lord? You know I've done my grieving and forgiving, but I'm still a bit ashamed and afraid of this monster secret.* The pressure wouldn't leave.

It's like Jesus said in Matthew 5: "You're here to be light, bringing out the God-colors in the world. God is not a secret to be kept. We're going public with this, as public as a city on a hill. If I make you light-bearers, you don't think I'm going to hide you under a bucket, do you? I'm putting you on a light stand. Now . . . shine!" (vv. 14–16 MSG)

Go public, Lord? How could you ask me to do this? But he did. Getting real about our junk prompts others to open up with God. I remembered what Women of Faith speaker and author Sheila Walsh said once, "My brokenness is a greater bridge to others than my pretend wholeness ever was."

Okay Lord. So with a cringe, the story went into the book. When I received Holly's e-mail I knew that my "Yes Lord, I'll do it your way" helped set her free to bring out the God-colors in her world.

King David's daughter Tamar never found that freedom and kept her light hidden under a bucket. Her story is a tragic tale that hits me in a tender spot. Though her half-brother Amnon told his friend, "I'm in love with Tamar" (2 Sam. 13:4), it was hardly love that drove him to assault her when she wouldn't give in. It was lust that soon turned to hate. Tamar's first response was the right one, unmasked and authentic grieving for her loss. "Tamar put ashes on her head and tore the ornamented robe she was wearing. She put her hand on her head and went away, weeping aloud as she went" (2 Sam. 13:19). Feeling the feelings is the starting place for freedom, but the guilt and anger can be so overwhelming that we disown them as a defense mechanism.

Tamar's brother Absalom later killed Amnon to avenge his sister, and he urged her, "Don't take this thing to heart" (2 Sam. 13:20). Easier said than done for poor Tamar. The worst crime—as some of us well know—was not being raped. We can survive the physical attack, but being betrayed by someone we trust, who violates us, is a monumental thing to get past.

Tamar did take the scandal to heart, she saw herself as spoiled goods and chose to retreat and live in Absalom's house, "a desolate woman" (2 Sam. 13:20).

There is always the Solomon-inspired time to reveal our secrets, but not when they're tender. If Tamar's story were a modern one, her retreat to her brother's house would be encouraged. Take some time, get over the shock, feel the feelings, get some good counsel, learn to forgive, and trust that God will restore what you've lost. The scandal and dishonor are not about you.

The closer we get to the Lord the more distinct will be his call to disclose our most inexpressible things. Like with me, his gentle voice urges when the time is "now." Thirty years after my "unfortunate incident" I finally shared my secret in a most public way. Prior to that I wasn't ready, nor was the Lord.

The word "secret" comes from the Latin *secretus*, which means "to set aside, to set apart." Our secrets set us apart from others, alienate us for fear we'll be found out. We dodge and change the subject; we avoid honest sharing . . . and maybe hide the family Bible.

When I was fifteen I went rummaging through my grandmother's desk for a tablet and came across the Hansen family Bible, with all the births and deaths recorded through generations of my family. Fascinating, especially the dated entry: *Newt marries Germaine.*

But, my mother's name is Alice.

I balked at the thought that my Daddy could have been married before. After demanding to know, my grandmother explained that his first wife divorced him while he was in the army during the early days of World War II. What a vital piece of my father's backstory that gave me a brighter picture of him.

It made me wonder what other family secrets lurked in desks and dark closets.

It turned out my mother had one, and it took her to the end of her days to reveal it. When my dad came down with terminal cancer, my mom refused to accept it and went into denial. Not me, though. I knew our time was short, so I spent every moment possible with him—in the garden letting him teach me about organic pest control, discussing world events, and getting his take on investments since he was so wise in that arena. It made him grin to hear "I love you, Daddy," and "I've learned so much from you." Nothing was left unsaid—even "I want to see you in heaven, Daddy." I'm not sure if he made a commitment, but my prayers were constant.

When he passed on in the middle of the night I was there, but my mom stayed home; she couldn't face losing her husband and anchor of forty-two years, and she was lost in a sea of grief.

Final arrangements were up to me. When my mother showed up tipsy, I planted a fake smile—the necessary kind for those occasions—and proceeded with the program to honor my father. After that, I wanted to strangle my mom. Instead, I invited her to church.

And she came. "I like the music," she said each week. Then one late winter morning she said "yes" to Jesus Christ, and soon after we had our first unmasked talk.

I had popped in on my way home from work to check on her. "Please sit down," she said taking a deep breath. Her eyes avoided mine, but somehow I sensed that the long awaited, fantasized-about-for-years, heart-to-heart with my mom had finally come. "I'm sorry—for the way I treated you all those years," she blurted.

Like a mountain stream, tears gushed down my cheeks as I held the frail and vulnerable woman in my arms. What courage it took for her to say this. I had forgiven her long ago for abandoning me emotionally. I'd let go of the childish hope that she would become the mother of my fantasies. But that day I saw God's full restoration at work.

She told me her backstory. Young Alice—fatherless since adolescence—worked as a stenographer in a small suburb of Boston to help support her widowed mother. It was the early 1940s, and she fell in love with a wealthy boy from the city. Staring at the floor she said, "I wasn't good enough for his family."

She choked on the next few words. "I got . . . pregnant, and his family told him if he married me they'd disinherit him. His parents paid for the . . . abortion."

Suddenly, all the pieces of the puzzle fell into place, the lost clues to my mother's mood swings. The good Catholic girl from New England had swept her shame under the rug, buried her past, bucked up, and went on with her life.

No wonder she jumped at the chance to marry my dad after the war, a GI she met on his way overseas, and escape to California. When I came along, her closely guarded secret sabotaged her happiness. She never healed from that experience, never resolved the guilt and anger, but instead retreated into her vodka. She couldn't enjoy the fullness of love my father offered, nor bond with her daughter, nor experience God's amazing grace and forgiveness.

One secret—well guarded—infected our family like a computer virus.

I'm sure she thought, what's the point in ever mentioning this unfortunate experience? But what if Mom had come clean with me years before and shared with her teenage daughter the disappointments and bad decisions in her life? Surely it would have torn down the walls between us and maybe helped me accept myself, uglies and all, and maybe I wouldn't have been so naïve as to put myself in a compromising situation and been so fooled by flattering words.

If ours were a house where honesty was welcomed, I may have turned to my parents first to work out problems as a family, knowing I wouldn't be condemned. Instead, I did what was modeled to me: denial and hiding. And the rest is history.

My mother's fierce protection of her secret tarnished the woman she was meant to be. Shame became her silent poison. That day, any remnants of my own pain and leftover dust of resentment ceased to exist as

God allowed me to see the woman behind the mask. Her drinking—and the nasty comments she hurled during her episodes—came from her own shameful backstory.

Once we see into someone's past and glimpse a heart imprisoned by disgrace, haunted by a guilty conscience, it's hard to hold a grudge any longer, even if we never hear the yearned for words, "Please forgive me." Bitterness is replaced with a longing for restoration to the Savior and the truth that sets them free.

Suddenly, I loved my mom.

But less than a year later, she gave up on life. "I just don't want to live without him," she kept insisting. Open and shut case. The doctor warned, "No more drinking. It will kill you," and despite my best efforts—*Mom, let's go on a cruise and have some fun*—her wish came true. Her liver gave out; she was just sixty-four years old.

My mother came to Jesus but never let him finish the work of transformation. For me, though, those lingering memories of her drinking binges are no more. When she comes to mind I see her in the kitchen whipping up a Boston cream pie to delight my friends, sewing me a pilgrim costume for the school play, designing my Junior Prom dress, or wrapping my head in a towel when she bleached my roots honey blond.

I may not remember many unsolicited "I love you's," but my mother showed her love the best she knew how with the creativity God gave her.

If she had lived longer, she would have basked in God's redemption. I wish she had fought as hard to live as she did to conceal her secret. Her shame could have become a giant billboard for Christ; she could have seen herself in the role of the Samaritan woman whose encounter with Jesus turned her life upside down. A woman with a whole lot of backstory, the Samaritan woman lived in isolation, probably on the outskirts of town, and ventured into the village to draw her water when the nice girls were not there, so she wouldn't have to face the scorn. One day she found Jesus who was asking her for a cup of water. *Me? A scandalous woman of mixed race. How can that be?*

As they chatted about religion, Jesus saw inside her soul and heard what she was really saying. He unmasked her on the spot ("You've had five husbands, and the man you're living with now isn't even your husband.") and tells her about the living water for which she is really searching (John 4:18–23 MSG).

Once Jesus revealed that he was the Messiah, she suddenly understood, dropped her water jar, dumped all her pretenses, disregarded her shame, and dashed to town shouting, "Come see a man who knew all about the things I did, who knows me inside and out" (John 4:29 MSG).

When you read about this encounter, notice how Christ asked her to receive him and his gift of living water without asking her to change. Trust always comes first, then the transformation.

Don't we constantly search for acceptance of who we really are, for forgiveness for the desperate decisions we've made? No sane woman wants the past to dominate and determine her future. She's just been playing the role far too long; it's become part of her.

When we claim our backstory, our secrets have no more power to hurt us. Pain loses its potency. Still, it's best to be wise about when, where, and to whom to reveal your story that will open the spiritual eyes of one who struggles with seeing the truth behind her shame.

Digging in Together

1. In light of 2 Corinthians 1:3–5, how does sharing from our painful places relieve the burdens of others?
2. In what ways have your body or your activities told you when you're trying to hold back pain?
3. Have you ever discovered a secret that shocked you? How did you respond?
4. Read Luke 8:16–17. What does this Scripture say about our lives? In what ways do these verses address the benefits of shedding our secrets?

Chapter 6

Pipe Dreams: Unrealistic Expectations

The first rule of acting is to be in the moment.

Godliness with contentment is great gain. (1 Timothy 6:6)

Decades past, when raising my toddler daughters, I tuned in to *Days of Our Lives* every afternoon, hooked on my favorite characters and their crises. It provided an escape from my routine as a young mom, home every day without a car. VCRs weren't the norm, so you couldn't tape your favorite episodes for later viewing. Everything came to a halt when that haunting voice said, "Like sands through the hourglass . . . so are the days of our lives."

As my girls grew, so did my penchant for daytime soaps. But then along came *Dallas* in the eighties, and I found myself rooting for Pam and Bobby to get back together and loving to hate JR. Nighttime soaps gave way to sitcoms like Seinfeld, so serial television lost its glamour to me. Until . . . I discovered *McLeod's Daughters,* an Australian show that follows five feisty women raising sheep and cattle in the outback.

And I'm hooked again. I tape every episode to watch at my leisure. I'm really into these characters. It's weird because they're so real to me, and they're only actors playing a role.

We love a good escape once in a while, as long as it doesn't get out of hand. Emma's tragic story comes to mind. As a young girl she devoured romantic novels and later saw marriage as the answer to her problems. But her new husband quickly grew dull and never measured up to her expectations of the gallant lover. So Emma retreated to her fantasy world of fiction where swashbuckling heroes whispered poetry in her ear. She longed for wealth, romance, and adventure like those promised in her books.

She searched for true love only to end up in dead affairs. In despair, she committed suicide.

Madame Bovary is a fictional story, so scandalous it was banned as immoral in the 1800s. In the1950s it became a movie, and I watched it a few months back on the classic movie channel. If it were set in modern-day USA, would we be shocked at Emma's folly, the way she chases an experience mistaking it for the ideal life? Or would we see a bit of ourselves in this poor girl, searching frantically for emotional intimacy and romantic satisfaction? Common sense tells us that romance won't bring us value, worth, and purpose, yet we still seek after perfect love.

We're women after all, raised on the happily ever after story.

As a hurting child, I too took shelter in the fantasy world of books and movies. Later, as a disenchanted wife, I read torrid romances of the strong yet vulnerable man tamed by the love of a good woman. And in my secret moments, when my troubled marriage thrashed my heart, I slipped into a fantasy about my first love, the one I let slip away. *If only I had waited for him, the country boy with the soul of a poet. He knew me so well. It was my ideal match, and he never would have thought of cheating on me, not coming from his strong, principled family.*

In a secret place I kept photos of us, a bundle of his letters, his photo on the sports page when he made the miracle play one night on the gridiron. Every now and then I'd peek at them, remembering the way he made me feel—pretty and funny and smart.

Once divorced, my fantasies about this man snowballed. Oh, I can admit it now, decades later, how I drove three hours to the mountain resort where we first met, just to have a mocha at what used to be the Frost Top hamburger joint where we poured quarters into the jukebox and played all the surfer songs. And how I stopped at the same cat then empty—that my parents rented each summer and sat in the old porch swing thinking of him, hearing our voices whisper so we wouldn't wake anyone up. Obsessed with finding him, I fantasized that he might have a few ruined dreams of his own. Perhaps he was staring up at the same moon toying with thoughts of what might have been. Maybe he loved the Lord.

Wouldn't that be a story only God could write? I really played this one out to the max.

My search ended promptly with the discovery through an old friend that my phantom hero was happily married and living out of state. *Let go, Jan.*

The thing about fantasies, what's missing in your life shows up in them. I spent my first marriage pretending my husband's affairs were just a phase, that he would grow out of his discontent—if I just loved him enough, if I became the woman of his sexual fantasies—and our story would contain a happily ever after because I'd make it happen. I'd be just like the heroines in my novels who finally overcame giant odds and found the perfect love.

And the dream died hard.

But fantasies are make-believe, illusions that must be exchanged for something real, something pure, something better. Fantasies can never satisfy. We will never outgrow our fascination with fiction, whether it's novels, plays, or movies. We enjoy being caught up into somebody else's story for a few hours. The challenge is to find the balance between the fantasies of the life we want and the realities of the life we have. It's learning to be okay with things we aren't really okay with. It's being gutsy enough to open yourself to the life God has given you.

Joan explains this well in an e-mail she sent me: "My parents were never satisfied with me, and I just wanted love, so I constantly chased relationships. Pretending men loved me was another lie I told myself. I had no friends. I didn't like myself, so I pushed people away if they dared come too close. While outwardly I was trying to do what normal people did, my real life was in my own universe. I pretended things were different than they were. In my mind I was in control of what was happening and what others would say or do. I was like a child with make-believe playmates. I refused to face reality. I lived a lie. I was a good actor, smiling on the outside while crying on the inside."

Joan admits she was quite a mess. "What God has done for me, and is still doing, is hard to believe. He opened my blind eyes, delivering me from the bondage of my own prison. I saw my past for what it was, not what I created it to be, and now it's where it belongs and doesn't hurt me anymore. I have learned to praise God for the things I had and what I didn't have. God is changing my whole outlook on life."

Joan first faced her feelings and owned her backstory. It's a continuing theme, isn't it? Then she reached out to God for understanding, ready to accept the truth.

The real and flawed world never meets our standards. Our real parents are far from perfect. Our flawed man can never live up to our expectations after the honeymoon, even if he is almost Mr. Wonderful. And our children will ignore the blueprint we've drawn up for their lives. And we're not happy. We tend to paint perfect people pictures and get deflated when they don't live up to our standards.

I call these our pipe dreams, an expression that my thesaurus dubs *a fantastic notion induced by smoking a pipe of opium.* I don't have to experiment with drugs to grasp that image. It about sums up a good fantasy, and the Devil can't wait to lure us into one.

For women, hoping for the ideal mate ranks high, especially for the kinds of lovers we meet in romance novels and movie theaters. Hollywood is a master at manipulating the emotions, and we are happy to spend nine dollars to let them do it.

One of the best examples of chasing a fantasy is Meg Ryan's character, Annie, in *Sleepless in Seattle,* one of my favorite chick flicks. She hears a widower, Sam, played by Tom Hanks, on late night radio. She's fixated on this mystery man and the way he describes the magical relationship he had with his wife, a magic missing for Annie. Think back on the scene when Annie and her best friend, Becky, are watching Cary Grant and Deborah Kerr in *An Affair to Remember.* With a wishful sigh, Annie says, "Now that was when people *knew* how to be in love." Becky tosses her a shrug. "That's your problem. You don't want to be in love. You want to be in love in a movie."

Bull's-eye, that hits me where I live.

The film ends with Annie's fantasy coming true—that's Hollywood—as she meets her mystery man at the Empire State Building. What woman doesn't give a big sigh at Sam and Annie's first meeting? I can watch that scene over and over, but it's still make-believe. We don't see the epilogue, what happens after the wedding. We don't see Sam after he's gained fifteen pounds on Annie's cooking, lounging on the couch flipping through the sports channels, and Annie wondering, is this the same guy I heard on the radio? How do I motivate him to mow the lawn?

If I had married my first love he would have done something dreadful—turned real on me. He would have changed into just an ordinary guy with quirks, habits, and hang-ups.

Romance is always destined to meet reality.

I love to share this concept at women's retreats, and it never fails that a woman like Tracy* will approach me. "My husband and I did it backward," she told me. "We had a baby first, then got married. We barely knew each other when I got pregnant, but we wanted to do the right thing." Her mate is not very romantic—or a deep thinker, as she hoped for—but after coming to the retreat she vowed to focus more on his positives, that he's a faithful Christian, a good provider and father. "I've been caught up in that fantasy of the ideal marriage," she admitted and vowed to return home and drop the pipe dreams. She will never have the ideal marriage. It does not exist, and the longer she pines for it, the more joy and contentment will elude her.

We can die to fantasies and they sneak back in.

One evening Carl offered to take me to a chick flick, so we chose *Shall We Dance*. Richard Gere's character, John Clark, is in a mid-life crisis. Because of his strange behavior his wife, Beverly (played by Susan Sarandon), thinks he might be having an affair and hires a private investigator. In truth, he's taking ballroom dancing lessons to spark up his mundane life. It's a delightful movie with a charming ending, and I left the theater swaying to the music, gazing into Carl's eyes with longing, certain he was about to say, "Honey, would you like to take a few ballroom dancing lessons?" After all, it was right before Christmas.

Nothing, not a word escaped from his lips. How unromantic, I thought. He knows I love to dance. I have rhythm in my soul, and I took up fishing for him. Why won't he stretch himself for me? I tumbled into bed in a huff.

In the morning I gave myself a mental shampoo. *Get a grip. You married a man with two left feet, but look at all the wonderful places they have walked with you.* I snapped myself out of my stinking thinking, surprised that I'd taken it that far.

We are so prone to overindulge our disappointments. We kick ourselves: *What's wrong with me that I'm never satisfied?* Think of Esther once she became the queen. Her marriage hardly resembled the one she dreamed about as a young Jewish girl. First, for Jews the responsibility for choosing a mate fell on your parents, who knew you the best. Esther landed her husband by untraditional methods, that's for sure. Second, in a Hebrew household the wife had traditional duties: cooking, making clothing, caring for children—again, not something that was part of Esther's life as a Persian queen.

And what about the quirky custom of keeping concubines, entirely legal but barbaric and certainly an evil in God's sight? I never went into my first marriage expecting to share my husband with other women.

Chestnuts Roasting

It's not just marriage hopes that need adjustment; how about holiday hopes? Am I the only one who can have a blue blue Christmas without much prompting? My most memorable childhood holidays were spent at my grandma's house with the entire family—aunts, uncles, cousins—squeezed around a lace-topped table. Yummy food, homemade eggnog, a cozy fire, Grandma pounding out yuletide carols on the organ, and endless party games. Nothing missing from these celebrations, except the snow.

But as Cheryl from my small group once said, "Christmas just isn't a Hallmark card."

Still, I tried to recreate Grandma's holidays for years without success. When Carl and I married I thought my expectations of what a second marriage would be like were on target. I knew the risks, challenges, and adjustments that would come.

But our blended family doesn't blend well. Our kids are grown and scattered and I am not the second mom to Carl's kids I imagined I'd be. Lots of warm fuzzies. Not quite yet, but I'm still hoping. For now, when "chestnuts roasting on an open fire" drifts through the department stores, it isn't Jack Frost nipping at my nose, but a little sadness and depression.

So I head for home and make a batch of English toffee and say to myself, "Snap out of it! Adopt a family; make it a Hallmark Christmas for them." And that works. And then I think of my dear friend Phyllis whose only child died in a car accident years ago, and while holidays are never easy, she still glows with love for Jesus, and her smile is not a phony front, it's real. And there's Margie, once a dynamo in tennis shorts, now in a wheelchair with multiple sclerosis. She wrestles daily with her limitations, sheds a tear now and then in frustration from trying to communicate with her disability, and smiles brighter than anyone I know because she is constantly looking for God's greater purpose.

Margie and Phyllis are my reality checks.

Life is never what we expect. We plan and dream but loved ones leave, we get passed up for the job, the medical test comes back bad and we're thrown off kilter. As Proverbs 19:21 says, you can make many plans, but the Lord's purposes will prevail.

There's nothing wrong with healthy desires—to be married if you're single, to move up in your career, to build a nest egg for your child's education, to beat the illness, to put on a nice holiday for your loved ones—but if these desires mushroom into obsessive fantasies, they are props that need to go.

Remember the Peanuts comic strip and picture Linus, constantly sucking his thumb, clasping a blanket to his cheek. "I can't live without that blanket!" he claims in one cartoon. "I can't face life unarmed." He might be where we got the term "security blanket." Our blankets are a symbol of what we stubbornly cling to. And to paraphrase Matthew 6:21, *Where your blanket is, there will your heart be also.*

Expecting Perfection: Even a Superwoman Can't Do It All

Scanning the *Sacramento Bee* recently I paused on a column called "The Sandwich Generation." The heading that day read, "Even a

Superwoman Can't Do It All, Nor Should She Try." The letter read: "I'm always running around for someone else. I never have time for myself. I'm getting tired, frustrated, and angry that no one thinks of me. I am not Superwoman. How can I find time to do what I want to do?"[1]

Carol, the columnist, urged the writer to put "no" on the top of her priority list. Simple enough solution, but some of us have been trying to do that for years and still can't figure it out.

Where did we collect the lie that we have to be perfect Christians? That having our act together is what counts to be effective for Christ? And if we just do enough good things and work harder for God we'll stay in his good graces. Welcome to the pipe dream of perfectionism. It begins with the mistaken belief that our worth is measured by performance.

God has never expected perfection from us, yet we strive in vain to achieve it. I read once—I'm constantly clipping insights from magazines without the source—that when you're exhausted and overwhelmed, your body is telling you that you are cast in a role you were not created to play. So that's what it is.

Nothing should pull us away from our best self, but striving to be Superwoman will do it every time.

Sue understands this. "I grew up thinking I had to earn love," she told me during breakfast one morning at a retreat. "When I recommitted my life to Christ I went in full swing as if to make up for lost time; I got involved in everything. It actually hurt my marriage because I was spending so much time doing God's work."

Sue found herself in deep depression, which happens when anger is turned inward. "And nobody knew it. I was afraid to admit it. In my quiet time one morning I asked God to tell me what I was afraid of, and the answer: *being me.* I was losing control, feeling so weak. Will they still love the woman who's vulnerable and not strong? I was raised to be strong and was angry because I was not. I lived in secret fear of failing so I was on a quest to succeed."

We show our shiny bumpers to each other, but not the dents, Sue says. We display our good sides, but hide our baggage in the trunk. Through a combination of small groups, biblical counseling, and friends, Sue learned to overcome her need to perform to be accepted.

She's a good example. The more we strive for perfection, the farther we lose ourselves. It takes powerful energy to make our world perfect, and our society reinforces hard work, personal sacrifice. We can become workaholics at church, around the house, as a mother. Why do we strive so hard? I have some theories: to numb our past hurts, to cover up our insecurities, to gain approval and appreciation, or because we don't know how to be good to ourselves and give ourselves permission to relax and play.

Striving for perfection is an energy that takes us from God's purposes. and into a world that swallows us up and melts us down. Then we think that seeking help, especially from a professional counselor, is a no-no. It means you're weak and can't manage your own life. Worse yet, you've failed spiritually and something is wrong if you can't go to the Scriptures and let Jesus the Counselor help you. Or it's too expensive and you're not worth it.

Rubbish to that. God created good counselors just as he did competent doctors and will use them as instruments to bring healing. Some women move beyond the masks on their own with Holy Spirit guidance, but some of us need a little jump start. And that's okay.

Some of us feel worthless if we're not producing. Our work ethic has been so instilled in us that we measure our worth by what we achieve. And we embrace the myth that we can have it all.

The world tells us success is all about performance, but God says it's all about relationship. As the psalmist said, "Going through the motions doesn't please you [Lord], a flawless performance is nothing to you" (Ps. 51:16 MSG).

My speaker friend Lil* discovered this earlier this year. "Lately, I've sensed God prodding me to be more honest when I speak," she told me. "While I've never presented myself as perfect or having it all together, I've never offered any evidence to the contrary." I asked her why. "I have some nasty stuff in my past, Jan, stuff that's really the biggest testimony of God's power, mercy, and grace in my life, but stuff I can't share publicly. It would hurt people I love. In the past, I've been at a loss as to how to share my real self with women, be open and vulnerable. I had the mistaken idea that in order to share, I had to share *everything*. As a perfectionist, I tend toward 'all or nothing' thinking."

medicine too

Who am I to talk, she wondered, compared to someone who's lost a child, survived incest or divorce. "My problems are nothing compared to what other women have experienced. Wouldn't they be offended at my whining about petty problems?"

Her former philosophy of life was to always put a smile on her face and never let on anything was ever wrong. "It's in my nature, part of my personality, so sharing from my weaknesses has been very difficult. This time, after talking to you about your book and the masks we wear, as well as wise words from another dear friend, I prayed about how to relate to these women."

To her surprise, God gave her a bounty of unmasked stories to share. "First, the loss of my writing dream, having to take a full-time job because of financial pressures. I added to that my struggles with losing weight, confessions of being a poor money manager, and goofs as a nurse at the hospital. Walls came down that weekend."

When one woman approached her with a raised eyebrow, Lil wondered if she'd gone too far. "When you first got up there on stage, I wasn't sure about you, but then I realized you were just like us."

Those are such magic words, *just like us.*

If Only. . .

It's tempting to think: If only I were married; if only I had more income; if only I had kids; if only my kids would behave; if only my husband were like hers . . . then I'd be happy.

We are always one step away from what we think will make us happy.

In my early single-again days there were a few weddings I didn't attend because I couldn't bear the agony of going alone. There were always those singles who wore the "super-spiritual" mask pretending they didn't desire a relationship with the opposite sex. If you're truly one with the Lord you don't have those desires.

Shame on me. Pile on more guilt.

Finally I figured out what contentment is. It's recognizing truth, accepting it, and living in the moment. My desire for remarriage never left—I saw myself as a partner for someone, serving the Lord as a couple—but my pipe dreams faded away, replaced by a real relationship

It's about looking peacefully at your future and knowing it's

with Jesus Christ. Contentment is helping plan a friend's wedding and not torturing yourself wondering if she'll ever be in your kitchen helping you with the same thing. It's being able to enjoy a friend's new house or celebrate her promotion or best selling book without yearning for it yourself. It's about looking peacefully at your future and knowing it's entirely in God's hands.

And he can handle it better than you.

Have you ever fantasized about the ideal love or recognition or success? Maybe it's financial freedom, and the good life, or peace amid the chaos. It's okay to daydream a little about a better life, but if it throws you off balance, stop and say, "Yes, I struggle with longings and slip into the occasional fantasy, and I am not going to kick myself for it. But today, I'm living in reality, in what's possible and practical for me. I won't ignore my emotions, but I won't let them overpower me either. I admit I'm broken and needy, and I'll deal with the fantasies one by one until they no longer have a hold on my heart."

Contentment is really a decision, I've found, not a feeling; it's a determination of the will, not a state of "higher consciousness." And everybody knows it has nothing to do with our circumstances. We can be content in spite of them. Maybe not jumping up and down with glee, but at peace with what is, even when we don't feel like it. I've had women admit to me that they put on a good face and call it contentment.

To be content is to find in Jesus a satisfaction so full that it fills up your heart and the aching corners of your soul.

The first rule of acting is to live in the moment. A good actor is focused on the here and now, ready for the unexpected, because it always happens. Every performance is different. A little glitch, a sudden surprise will throw her off if she is mindlessly delivering her lines, thinking about tomorrow or yesterday. Acting is all about communicating with her partners on stage, responding to them as if it were the very first time. When the unexpected comes, she's ready to be impromptu.

For us, it means readjusting our expectations daily, hourly if we need to. And it's waking up every morning knowing God may have something planned that's different than what we expect. It's making a choice to be content with whatever today holds.

Surprise me, Lord.

entirely in God's hands.

Digging in Together

1. What is your favorite romantic movie and why? In what ways is it a commentary on life as it is? In what ways does it fantasize love and relationships?
2. Describe a magical time in your childhood. What made it so? Have you tried to recapture that magic as an adult? Has it worked?
3. Share one of your pipe dreams, past or present.
4. Read Matthew 6:1 and compare Jesus' statement to Paul's in Ephesians 2:8–9. In what ways have you worn the perfection mask?

Chapter 7

Stage Fright

Everybody gets first night jitters. Find a way to use them.

I sought the Lord, and he answered me;
he delivered me from all my fears.
(Psalm 34:4)

I'm not letting any man control me. I'll *never* put a man first ever again."

Whoa, Mary Gail. Where is this coming from? And then it made sense. My friend is a locust survivor like me, once married to a critical man who also left her for another woman. She had worked as a home school consultant for our rural school district to support her three children, now grown and out on their own. She had one post-divorce relationship—a disaster—and that convinced her she was a flop when it came to men.

Faulty logic and fear brought on a big case of stage fright.

"I'll never get married," she vowed many times, yet of all the singles in our fellowship Mary Gail was a born helpmate. But to me and Jeanne she would say, "I'm just not cute and fun like you two." The compare and compete game anyone?

Then she met Hal, a widower, one of our church elders and the adult Sunday school teacher, and friendship grew into strong attraction. She tried hard to stem the tide of her feelings. "What could I possibly offer this man? I have no assets," she said to me.

"Except those that count," I argued and rattled off the fruit of the Spirit of Galatians 5: love, joy, peace, patience, kindness, goodness, faithfulness, gentleness and—"Okay, forget self-control. We all struggle with that."

My friend had fallen for the lie that her worth was measured by her material assets and physical appearance. She wasn't pretty or clever enough and had nothing tangible to bring into a marriage, translated to mean, "I'm really not woman enough for him."

After hashing this out she finally admitted, "Hal truly cares about me. He thinks I'm wonderful. I've never experienced this before, and it's very scary."

No doubt. It's much more comfortable to remain in the deception, to keep a padlock on the heart, than to risk breaking through the fear and getting to the other side where clarity dwells.

Finally she emerged from her fog. "If this relationship is of God, I really don't want to throw it away. I'll take a step and get to know him a little better."

A few months later, she sent me an e-mail: "On a deep level, I'm beginning to open up to Hal. I thought I was healed from my marriage and forgiven for my past, but there are still wounds there. I see now that I've pushed down who I really am as a woman. God is telling me I have to risk being me, no matter what happens."

Mary Gail already possessed everything she needed to be a life partner for Hal, but fear and faulty thinking screened out the truth. When she risked being authentic, she confronted her fears and long-held doubts. As she felt genuinely loved, she grew lighter in spirit and more certain of herself as a woman. Life is never without risk. Mary Gail dared to dance on the edge, and last year she married Hal and they make a good team serving the Lord.

Fears flee when we confront them.

For a long time I feared for my daughter Amy. At the end of her prodigal years she married in haste and before long decided she'd made a big mistake. She called me every day from her home in Southern California crying spastic tears. If you're a mom you know what it's like to fear for your child—for me it was that she'd be trapped in a difficult marriage, a fear that saturated and strangled my heart because of my own backstory. My imagination ran wild with all the possibilities, magnified ten times over.

Fear is a twin sister to worry, but I'd been waylaid at this whistle stop before when Amy would be gone for weeks at a time as a young teenager. Keeping busy helped, but I always had that pit-of-the-stomach sensation that disaster was about to strike. I came across a book by Dale Carnegie from 1948 called *How to Stop Worrying and Start Living*—a classic still in print—and the only thing I remember was this: Ask yourself, what is the worst thing that can possibly happen? Can you live with it?

The worst was that I'd get a call from the police and know she was never coming home. I had to stare fear point blank in the face and ask: Can I accept being crushed by this? Can I trust that God is in control no matter what? A tough question for any situation, but if the answer is yes it breaks the handcuffs—and the heart chain—of fear. It's shoring yourself up with Romans 8:28 yet again. God works all things together for good . . . without fail.

And always, on the other side of fear is freedom.

One tense morning in my prayer time for Amy and her marriage woes, I flung open the floodgates admitting my newest fears to God. I turned to the Psalms. "I sought the LORD, and he answered me; he delivered me from all my fears" (Ps. 34:4). I'm not consistent with my journal, but I did jot down my thoughts that day. "I hear you speaking to me, Lord, through this verse, with a promise that you will deliver me from my fears, fears about Amy's marriage. I cast them on you, hard as it is, because I know you are close to the broken-hearted, and I am so broken-hearted today. My spirit is crushed from the weight of it. But you are greater than my fears."

Most fears are useless. Ninety percent of the things we worry about never happen, yet we poison our contentment with fear of the big shipwreck. We imagine it in living color on a giant screen plasma TV with surround sound.

In time, God worked in Amy's marriage and used their troubles for good.

Our worries are hard habits to break. Corrie ten Boom, who spent years in a Nazi concentration camp, said worry is like a rocking chair—it keeps you moving but it doesn't get you anywhere.[1] It just wears a rut on your porch and one day you'll fall right through. And as my grandmother used to say, worry is as useless as a handle on a snowball.

We worry about not having enough to pay the bills, we fret about our kids, about growing older, of ending up alone and abandoned. We fear failure or that life will pass us by. We're frightened of the future, so we hide in the past. We're scared of what makes us different, so we follow the crowd.

And there's nothing like the anxiety of finding a suspicious lump.

My friend Laura Jensen Walker battled this. When the doctor said those frightening words "breast cancer," she cried what she calls tears of terror. Only then could she survey all the options with husband Michael. They decided on a mastectomy and heavy, heavy dosages of chemotherapy, which Laura talks about in her book, *Thanks for the Mammogram*.

This nightmare no woman wants to wake up in had an upside. It taught Laura to confront her fears head-on. "One in every eight women will get breast cancer," she says. "Yes, that's frightening, but it's a fact. Hiding from it won't change that. Even more frightening to me is the fear. It's fear that prevents women from getting lumps checked. Fear that she'll be less of a woman without a breast. Fear of the effects of chemo. Fear that she'll be unattractive without hair."

Hair grows back, she says. Your life doesn't.

I'll never forget my suspicious lump and the sheer panic between the discovery and the biopsy. Waiting for the results, I wrote out my memorial service. I've never been so scared.

It's been said that fear and anxiety kill as many women as the number of men that die on the battlefield. An astounding thought. There are no statistics to back this up, but we know that nearly twice as many women in America die of heart disease and stroke than from cancer, including breast cancer. One in every three of us will battle heart disease.

Could there be a connection between worry and stress? Okay, the reports state that the leading cause of heart attacks in women are smoking and being overweight, but what mentally sound woman doesn't know the dangers of smoking? But it's a habit, a way of life. Although I've never been a smoker I have known gals who gave up cigarettes, but the minute they're under stress, they grab for one to cope. "It calms the qualms," one friend said.

And the cycle starts all over again.

We women are more stressed today than ever, and some of us turn to food. I confess, I'm a stress muncher. As long as the pond is still—no ripples—I go for the balanced meal, low fat and healthy, but the minute the wind kicks up and the waves of worry threaten to hit, I head for the kitchen for something to crunch on. And it's never celery. No, I need crackers or cookies and I never stop at just one. And I'm a closet eater at that. I hide the evidence so Carl doesn't suspect I've been on a blue funk binge.

He never seems to notice my expanding tummy, bless his heart.

Our bodies are a bench mark of what's going on underneath. We'll all have a physiological reaction—sooner or later—to the stress in life; our blood pressure spikes, we get ulcers and headaches. Some of us live so edgy and uptight but never know it until a friend gives us a gift certificate for a full body massage and we're surprised to hear the therapist say, "Your muscles are so bound up."

Some of our fears come from wanting to be perfect, to get it right and not let others down. So we pile on more responsibilities and panic at the thought of backing out on our commitments. We worry, what will others think? If we can only get rid of the mask and admit we can't do it all, and we are never going to be perfect, it takes mega pressure off ourselves.

Worry is a waste and there is no profit in it. And if you're a brooder, you may find it tough to trust God, that he can take charge. Jesus says, "Don't fuss about what's on the table at mealtimes or whether the clothes in your closet are in fashion. There is far more to your life than the food you put in your stomach, more to your outer appearance than the clothes you hang on your body" (Matt. 6:25 MSG). And this is great: "Has anyone by fussing in front of the mirror ever gotten taller by so much as an inch?" (v. 27 MSG).

But how do we slow down this train of troubles? Jesus gives us the answer: "steep your life in God-reality" (MSG) the short and sweet version of "Seek first his kingdom and his righteousness, and all these things will be given to you" (Matt. 6:33).

And the Lord goes on to urge us not to worry about tomorrow because today has enough troubles of its own. She who fears the future may not enjoy the present.

Fear comes from uncertainty. I like what Marie Curie said: "Nothing in life is to be feared. It is only to be understood."[2] Born with a brilliant aptitude for study, Marie's thirst for knowledge hit a drought after being denied admission into Polish universities because of her gender. But did she let that detour her dream? No, she found her way to France, married Pierre, gained her Doctor of Science degree and became the first woman to teach in that university. She and Pierre devoted their lives to research in a basement laboratory studying radioactive materials. They went on to discover radium and Marie won two Nobel Prizes, the first woman to receive that honor. After Pierre's tragic death, she continued alone. Imagine where modern science would be if her fears held her back.

She is so right, we fear the unknown, what lies around a dark corner.

Anna Sewell, author of *Black Beauty,* one of my beloved children's stories, spent most of her life as an invalid. By the time she reached middle age she could no longer leave the house, but did she retreat in self-pity? No, she spent her time writing a story about a mistreated horse. She faced her limitations and fully accepted them, and she echoed Marie Curie when she said, "I am never afraid of what I know."[3]

And what I know is that life is uncertain. Fear comes when we want to know how it all turns out, like reading the end of the book before the first chapter. We must let go of life on our own terms and replace our fears with faith. Okay, it's a stock answer, but it's true.

We need to come face to face with our fears or we'll run away from them. It helps for me to talk about what's troubling me. Keeping the lid on uneasiness can cause depression as we press down our worries to keep them out of sight. If something is on your mind—maybe your workload, your children, your mate or lack thereof, or your health—take the risk and talk it out with somebody.

Fears spring from ignorance and faulty thinking. Stage fright comes when we rehearse the wrong lines: "I've messed up and God will never bless me. I'm doomed, but I'll put on the happy face and pretend I'm content settling for less." "God isn't listening to me anymore. He's forgotten about me." And when disaster strikes, we wonder whether it may be a punishment from God because of unconfessed sin or a weak prayer life. We come into the Christian life with superstitions and wrong beliefs that have to be set right. We've talked about this. God's very nature is goodness. "The LORD is good to all; he has compassion on all he has made" (Ps. 145:9).

On the flip side is the belief that, "Of course God will bless me. I've been through so much. He will reward me." We're viewing it with a blind eye if we use that logic. "Since God is good and desires to bless me, He will give me ————." You fill in the blank, a new house, wonderful husband, healing for my friend.

And this one, "Nothing bad will ever happen to me now that I'm a Christian." Then it does and you begin to doubt and worry. Of course God has good things in store for us, a harvest of blessings—but blessings defined by him, not us. It's the spiritual harvest that we should seek, the harvest that can never be destroyed. It's not wrong to hope and dream for a new job after a layoff, a nice house when we have to move, a good husband, a healing, but to expect specific blessings from God is a setup for frustration.

All actors get fearful and nervous before the show, if they're honest. Despite how many times I've walked on stage to do my thing at a women's retreat, I still get the "first night jitters" before I begin. The trick is to expect and accept them. When I first started speaking, I'd take a deep breath and ask myself, what are you actually frightened of? Having nothing to say? Turning into a jibbering wreck? Making a fool of yourself? Any of these things might happen, especially in my line of work. Somehow those are the most memorable moments in the weekend.

Asked how he remembered all his lines in a one-man show, a famous actor said, "By forgetting everything else." What's important here is mind-set. Not to fear what could go wrong, but to be in the moment and enjoy it.

Good things can come from fear, and there is time to take counsel in them. Healthy fear protects us, keeps us watchful of the heart and home. And as a wise mentor once said, a good scare is worth more than good advice sometimes. "The fear of the LORD is the beginning of wisdom" (Ps. 111:10).

And if you find yourself at your wits' end, that's not a bad thing. It's just where God lives.

Digging in Together

1. As we grow from child to woman, we pick up attitudes and beliefs that God wants us to unlearn when we become his. See Colossians 2:8. Share an attitude, expectation, or opinion about the Christian life you've had to unlearn.
2. It has been said that F.E.A.R. is False Evidence Appearing Real. What are your greatest fears right now?
3. What are the signs that you're worrying too much?
4. How can Matthew 6:34 affect our trust?
5. When have you taken a risk on faith?

Chapter 8

Stealing the Show

We upstage God when we insist on the limelight.

Pride first, then the crash. (Proverbs 18:12 MSG)

There is no such thing as a self-made woman. In the quest for rising star status it's too easy to trip in the limelight. During my early unmasking I went from selling myself short to patting Jan on the back a bit too much. That's what a few successes—a few shouts of "Bravo!"—will do for you. The "well dones" came from others—recognition at my legislative job and as a singles ministry leader—and from me, congratulating myself that I finally set some boundaries and learned to say no.

But most of the "three cheers for you, Jan" popped up on my trips to the do-it-yourself store. After losing Mr. Fix-it, I traded shopping at the mall for browsing the home improvement stores, buying tools. On Saturdays I attended all the free how-to seminars, and instead of dozing off with a good novel at night I fell asleep to instruction manuals.

My house needed repairs, so any weekend you could find me tearing off paneling, replastering walls, caulking leaky windows. I was the do-it-yourself queen, and when a few handy men in our singles group offered to assist gals whose places needed patching, I snickered with pride that I would never be one of them.

Then my friend Jeanne bought her first solo house, the best she could afford on her teacher's salary. What the realtor described as a true "vintage charmer," I saw as a "perpetual fixer-upper." I could hear the sound of sinking savings, thousands of dollar bills floating out the old double-sash windows.

"Are you sure you want to tackle this?" I asked. "What happens when things break? You don't own a single tool." Now Jeanne is no giddy-head, but when it comes to tools, she is purposefully ignorant and calls them "gizmos" and "whatsits."

She rolled her eyes. "Now, what would I need tools for? I have you, the Mistress of Maintenance."

Flattery will get you anywhere, so when Jeanne summoned me for a service call, I dashed over with my little red toolbox. Together—she handed me another "doohickey" and a home-baked cookie—we fixed the front porch light, mended the swamp cooler, patched the roof, and stopped countless window leaks.

We'd grin at each other and chirp, "We're so good. Who needs a man?" When first single, I felt like unfinished furniture without a man around, but it was different now. I'd found treasure inside my toolbox waiting to unleash its power like the genie in Aladdin's lamp. The little red toolbox became a symbol of my new resolve, proof that living well is the best revenge.

There was almost nothing I couldn't fix. *I am woman. I have tools. I am invincible.*

Until one night around ten o'clock when I received a frantic call, "Jan! Help! I locked myself in the bathroom. I climbed out the window to call you, and I need you over here fast. The door won't budge." Toolbox in tow, I arrived a few minutes later, ready to roll up my sleeves again, eager to solve Jeanne's problem and be back before the late news.

But, this time Wonder Woman hit a slight snag. None of my incredible state of the art tools could unjam the door. My hammer and chisel wouldn't take off the hinges either; a half century of paint stood in my way. "This is a bigger task than I thought," I hated to admit. In desperation I pulled out my cordless drill. As the new tool hummed, Jeanne screamed in protest. "Stop! I'll have to replace the entire door. It's original and an odd size. I'll never find another one."

"Do you have to consider historical preservation at a time like this?"

My drill went silent. It was now eleven o'clock, and Jeanne's only entrance to the bathroom was to climb through the window. Isn't it amazing how much we take our little conveniences for granted?

I cringed at what I was about to admit. "Well, Jeanne, it looks to me like we're licked and we only have one option."

"No . . . not that. Really? Are you serious?"

"Yes, I'm afraid so. I hoped it would never come to this, but I'm afraid . . ." I choked, "we have to call a man."

We laughed at our dismay over this. We only knew one guy who stayed up that late, so we called Richard. He arrived in his sweats and ball cap ten minutes later. "So—the dynamic duo finally summons help," he said with raised chin and bloated chest. "You can't know how long I've waited for this."

"Just get on with it please," I said. "But where are your tools?"

"Don't need any." He sauntered up and down the hallway a few times, glancing my way. "Just watch this, girls." He flipped out his pocketknife, slipped it between the door and the lock, and it swung free. "Works every time."

My head hung like a naughty puppy and my face turned as red as my toolbox. They just don't teach you how to open doors with pocketknives at the home improvement store.

Okay, I'd swung too far with my do-it-yourself confidence and let it deceive me. Real strength is admitting you can't do it yourself and reaching out for help when you need it. God used a man and his pocketknife to shave off the "I'm the greatest" mask.

And Richard has never let us forget what he calls the "Bathroom Caper." Years later when Carl and I invited guests to share thoughts and reflections at our wedding reception, Richard came forward with a page full of notes. He recounted the entire story to the whole crowd, complete with a few embellished details. "I hope I didn't embarrass you too much," he said to Jeanne and me later, "but that night was one of the highlights of my life."

For our first anniversary I asked Carl for my own toolbox—red of course—to remind me that God does not cast us in one-woman shows; a reminder of the time I got too big for my overalls.

Pride is our biggest hindrance. It's at the root of all our sin. A barrier

"You know you want to" — Satan

to forgiveness, it blinds us to our faults. Because of it we stumble over the truth, and so effortlessly at times.

We make the mistake of thinking, "I've arrived." Or we slip on the mask of "I deserve it." I've worked hard and done my part and life should revolve around me for a change. I think of Satan, once a leading player in heaven, until pride came on the scene.

It's a seductive thing.

We carry around our soapbox, ready to launch into an impromptu speech, calling it *encouragement.* I still catch myself dispensing some of my hard-fought wisdom when nobody has asked for it, when all a woman wanted was to get something off her chest. Like my husband Carl always tells me, "Unasked for advice is veiled criticism." Ooh, that stings. Throwing Scripture verses at the wounded—with a kindly pat on the back—is like saying, "Read your Bible like I do. Be a spiritual giant like me, and then you won't have any more trouble."

Not to say we don't share God's Word with good intentions—to help others and save them the grief because we've already learned how to handle it—but when we rattle off our top ten Scripture verses, "Just remember what Jesus said . . ." we're still belting out a mini-sermon. Preaching *at* the wounded is the lazy way and pride is at its root. Listening to what someone is really saying takes time and effort. It translates to mean: Your feelings are important to me. "Would you like to pray about this?" is a preferable response because most of us, unfortunately, learn truth the hard way.

After you pray with her, if she asks your opinion about her situation—or the jam she's in—offer it with love. Look what Paul tells the Galatians: "If someone falls into sin, forgivingly restore him, saving your critical comments for yourself. You might be needing forgiveness before the day's out. Stoop down and reach out to those who are oppressed. Share their burdens, and so complete Christ's law. If you think you are too good for that, you are badly deceived" (Gal. 6:1–3 MSG).

And another self-deceit is thinking, "God loves me and he understands what I'm doing, and he'll forgive me, so that makes it okay." Welcome to more faulty thinking. Yes, God loves us so much that he never gives up trying to make us right with him, and *nothing* escapes his scrutiny. If necessary, he'll bring us back again and again—and yet again—to the same point until we learn the lesson, no matter what it takes.

Discipline is a sign of love, any mother knows that. "No discipline is enjoyable while it is happening—it is painful! But afterward there will be a quiet harvest of right living for those who are trained in this way" (Heb. 12:11 NLT). If you have a friend who's trapped in sin, who's living outside the will of God, pray about whether you are the one to speak the truth in love to her. God may use you to open her heart, but if the timing is wrong it could backfire on you. Then again, the timing could be perfect, and her response may be less than kind.

I've been in both places.

Because of my ministry women call me, write me, approach me at conferences with questions, but mostly, "I need a word of encouragement for what I'm going through." They've read my books or heard me on the platform for a few hours, sharing my stories and the lessons from the locusts in my life. I'll never see most of these women again and some of them are at the crisis point. My first thought is to dish out advice, but I don't know all of their backstory. The best thing I can do is wrap my arms around them and pray, or send a cheerleading note. I'm just a germ of a seed of truth that floats through their life. I am not the answer.

Something to remind myself of daily. It's so easy for me to slip into spiritual pride because of all the mountains I've climbed in my Christian trek. I speak and write books that urge Christians to stand on the promises, to live in the light of the truth. But I'm still trekking and God isn't finished with me yet. I constantly have to ask the Holy Spirit what I need to deal with, what confessions I need to make, and what cleansing and unmasking need to go on inside me.

And the answer never fails to come in brilliant color. Pride and God's spirit are incompatible.

Pride's twin may be impatience. We get antsy in God's waiting room, don't we? When God doesn't intervene as we think he should we fidget. *I can't just sit here, I have to make something happen in this situation.* Keep in mind, this is exactly what the Devil wants, for us to move ahead of God and find ways to fix the problem in our own strength.

As my friend Wendy says, most of us are uncomfortable with *becoming.*

We don't like the idea of God peeling away our protective coating. We cringe at being exposed, and it hurts. We'd rather get busy, making things happen, and then we don't have to deal with the hard stuff.

Does anyone do waiting well? We check our watch in traffic, fidget in grocery store lines, and hope the stylist hurries up at the beauty parlor so we can get to our next appointment.

We blurt, "I'm such a busy bee these days." Well, bees may buzz around, but if you study their lifestyle, they are not into multitasking. Each bee knows its function and purpose and attends to it, giving its very best. We can learn from those little bees; the process from gathering the pollen to creating the honey takes time.

The sign of maturity is accepting delayed gratification. This kind of patience really scares the enemy. He goes to work on us with subtle charm. Like the Pied Piper—from the Robert Browning poem—who offers himself as the savior of the town from its rat problem. He plays a haunting tune on his pipe and the rodents march behind in fascination, following him to their deaths in the river.

We are prone to follow such a tune to our spiritual deaths in the river of self-satisfaction.

Our most costly mistakes are made when our heart is anxious and impatient.

Whenever I think of "patience" an Italian ceiling pops into my head. On our honeymoon trip to Europe, I began reading a biographical novel about Michelangelo. By the time we toured the Sistine Chapel in Rome, I felt this guy's agony at being forced to sideline his dream of sculpting— bringing slabs of marble to life—in order to paint the Sistine Chapel ceiling. In those days you didn't buck the Pope when he commissioned a project, and this was a monumental one. It took Michelangelo four long years, lying flat on his back on a scaffold, his body wracked with pain.

But the end result sends chills down your spine. Staring up to view God's hand reaching out to give Adam life in the "Creation of Man," you cannot help but see the inspired genius in it. You realize what this man's suffering produced. Irving Stone titled his book *The Agony and the Ecstasy,* and I can see why. From Michelangelo's agony—the task that nearly did him in—comes ecstasy for millions five hundred years later.

Our visit came not long after restoration of the ceiling, which took fourteen years. The scholars were shocked. Centuries of grimy varnish had dulled the artwork and masked the true colors Michelangelo had created, the vibrant blues and reds, vivid oranges and yellows.

Life has a way of piling on the crud, hiding our brilliance, but if we're patient God will shine us up again. There are no wonder-working formulas. Still, we search for the quick fix, the next new life-changing book, seminar, or infomercial. But growing into a godly woman occupies an entire lifetime.

Progress drags its feet sometimes and resembles our childhood game of Chutes and Ladders, with giant strides toward the goal, and then oops, a slide back down to where we started. There's no way to schedule spiritual growth spurts in our day planners.

Patience is the name of this game.

Michelangelo could have completed the Sistine Chapel ceiling in a year if he wanted. He could have rushed the job to fulfill his contract so he could get on with pursuing his own dreams. After all who would know? But to be true to himself and the gift God gave him, he wouldn't settle for anything less than his ultimate best . . . even if it killed him.

Patience personified.

Waiting on the Lord is one of the hardest things we have to do. I've died to many of my dreams and visions over the years because I pursued them in my own strength, tried to make things happen before their time. Once I let them go and couldn't swell with pride that I did something wonderful, I saw God resurrect them again.

The temptation to strive and overextend will always stare us in the face. We can't all live in convents, but we can take a retreat, not to the shopping mall or into a box of chocolates, but to Daddy's lap, as he holds us near and gets our heartbeat back in sync with his.

When we're too busy God always gives us warning signs. For me it's a flare-up in my left jaw, something the dentist calls TMJ. It's an inflammation of the jaw joint caused—surprise, surprise—by grinding my teeth at night many eons ago, in the days when I wore the "everything is fine" mask but took my anxiety to bed with me.

On occasion the jaw speaks with searing pain and I have to ask: *Okay, where am I off beam?* So it's time to get back in the eye of the tornado once again. That's the way I describe solitude with God.

People who've survived being swept into a twister say that the center glows and the silence is incredible. It's the place to be when the world is crashing in. In silence God speaks most clearly. "The Spirit helps us in our weakness. We do not know what we ought to pray for, but the Spirit himself intercedes for us with groans that words cannot express" (Rom. 8:26).

A quiet moment with God allows us a good drink of the living water that never dries up. It's the place where God can strip away our blinders and take the wax out of our ears.

In the theater, when actors aren't onstage bringing a story to life, they might be found hanging out in the green room. It may be painted blue, but it's still called the green room. It's where the actors can go to relax and take a deep breath before they get back into character. Your green room, wherever it may be, is where you gain control over your hectic life, downshift, slow down, return to your core. Accept the fact that some things you've been doing are done with the wrong motivations.

For years now I've served on faculty at a local writers' conference. My chance came when one of the regular, more experienced writers couldn't teach her workshop, and would I fill her slot? You bet, and who cares that I was second fiddle yet again. This was my "in." There are perks attached to this: it looks great on your professional resume and you get to rub shoulders with other writers, it's like a big literary party.

And you know how I love parties.

Last year when asked what workshops I'd be doing, I knew my heart was not in doing it. I had a book deadline and speaking engagements, and yet I couldn't let go. So many writers want to be workshop teachers, and if I don't come one year I'll never get back in. *Now, Jan let's examine what this really is.*

You guessed it. Pride again. And when I took a hard look and asked myself, does this fit into God's plan for my life right now, the answer had to be no. I'm busier now than ever, and something has to give. So last week when I got the call, I declined. And no regrets, no secret yearnings. It's time to move on and make choices that positively impact the way I live.

There's such freedom in knowing our limits and being bold enough to change direction.

If I didn't take time to regroup and take inventory, I'd never have come to this conclusion. Now I'm learning to practice the three D's.

> **D**elegate—you can't do everything.
> **D**o your best and drop the rest.
> **D**ownsize—dump the things that stand in
> your way of gleaming for God.

So if you are overwhelmed, survey your commitments. Sometimes the way to get everything done is knowing what to leave undone.

Digging in Together

1. What do you think of the idea that God will bring us back to the truth by whatever means it takes? What point have you had to come back to more than once? Share an insight from the experience.
2. Which of your strengths make you most proud?
3. In what ways does pride seduce you?
4. What giant spiritual strides have you made only to slide back down to where you started?
5. Read James 1:2–4. What is the role of patience in this process of growth? Read Paul's hope for the future in 2 Timothy 4:5–8. How does this challenge you right now?

Chapter 9
The Mimic

Be an original, not a copy.

This world is fading away, along with everything it craves. But if you do the will of God, you will live forever. (1 John 2:17 NLT)

Becoming a feminist was easy for Barbara Curtis. She just tossed out her bra, got a tattoo, and tried some LSD. I met Barbara at a writers' conference and couldn't believe this all-American mom was an ex-hippy. Talk about transformation. As we chatted about her book about culture clashes—working title: "Reaching the Left with the Right"—I asked if I could pick her brain a little. Barbara is an expert in the area of transformation.

In the sixties she devoured the best-seller *The Feminine Mystique* by Barbara Friden. "I identified with the frustration with the hats we women wear: wife, lover, mom, chauffeur," she said. "And I was one of those gals afraid to ask the question, is this all there is? But I secretly wondered all the time."[1]

The idea that God created men and women differently made no sense to her. "I thought it was all social conditioning." She rallied behind feminism and everything it embraced. After a painful divorce, she met Tripp and they became New Age seekers. "We each had embarked on a solo search for the truth years before," she said. "We meditated together daily. In emptying our minds to achieve higher spiritual realms, we even had visions of our past lives which reinforced our feeling that we truly belonged together."

Friends and family tried to warn them to slow down. "After all, I had two daughters from my first marriage, and Tripp, seven years younger, had little history of responsibility. How could he take on a ready-made family?" Against advice, they eloped and married at sunset on the California coast. "An innkeeper dutifully intoned passages containing all the muddled theology we had so far pieced together," Barbara added.

When designing the wedding announcements, she hunted through her spiritual books for a suitable quote and dug out a dusty Bible. "I treasured the gilt-edged book like my crystal collection or the pictures of various spiritual masters arrayed on our meditation altar, including Jesus. We thought of him as a great teacher worthy of our attention. Believing that *all* paths led to the same God, we thought Christians were misguided and narrow-minded. They didn't understand the esoteric, or hidden, message behind the things Jesus said. Being more advanced spiritually, we understood Jesus to be a more highly evolved being who had tried to show us that we are all divine.

"This Jesus and the Father being one thing, I thought he was trying to show us that we are *all* God. Tripp and I wanted more than anything to achieve our divine potential." They delighted in New Age ideas and practices.

With the addition of three sons, they had five healthy children and looked like a wholesome, happy, and successful family. "People looked to us for advice and encouragement in their own lives."

So what's the flaw in this picture? "Tripp and I, each *seemingly* so in harmony with the universe, could not achieve harmony in our marriage. We argued about everything." Neither money, success, nor achievement helped. "We were stubborn, strong-willed people. Believing in our own divinity only made matters worse. How could two gods ever live happily under the same roof?

"The New Age movement had taught me nothing about submission or compromise; instead, it had assured me of my right to be happy. I decided I had made a mistake. Tripp was not my soul mate, after all."

As Barbara tuned in Christian radio for parenting advice, God tugged at her heart. "Just when I was ready to give up on my marriage, I heard Dennis and Barbara Rainey on *FamilyLife Today* plugging their marriage conferences. In a last-ditch effort to save ours, I signed us up for the following weekend."

In the opening session they heard strange concepts, such as the family is God's building block and "Satan is out to destroy it."

What an eye opener. Could this be a spiritual battle, she wondered? She and Tripp decided to burn their meditation altar and rid their home of New Age books, tapes, pictures, and idols, and became avid Bible readers. "Gone were our beliefs in astrology, reincarnation, and pantheism. We found a church that taught God's Word clearly and entered there as babes, not as the highly evolved spiritual beings we had thought ourselves to be."

And the bitterness toward her husband was gone too.

Barbara is now speaking out on the danger in the world's teaching. "Today's young woman is brought up to think she can have it all. Instead of being encouraged to become wives and mothers, women are pushed to have careers, gain more power, and squeeze in marriage and family if she has the time or inclination. Many new mothers are surprised when after a six-week maternity leave, they want to stay home."

As Barbara came to understand the biblical concept of marriage—to give up her struggle for control and be a partner—she started meeting Christian women in the opposite camp. "They're not only trying to run the show at home but at church too, and it throws a family off balance."

I've seen it. In my early Christian days, it was men who left the family for the most part, but in the last decade women are ending marriages to their believing—but flawed—husbands because things just aren't working. One gal told me, "Next time I want a stronger spiritual leader in the home."

Huh? And God's okay with that? I have seen a woman toss out her wedding ring, insisting, "I do love God, but he wouldn't want me to be unhappy."

Sounds like a severe case of faulty thinking to me.

The Barna Group, an independent Christian based market research company in California, states that many Americans have fallen in love with faith, rather than the object of their faith. "It's much less demanding to be devoted to the idea of faith than to invest yourself in a true relationship with the living God."[2]

True relationships demand total honesty—no masks, no games—and many Christians are not ready for that, so they play church and pretend to be faithful.

Believers should stand firm in marriage not because we have the ideal mate—that's a pipe dream—but out of obedience to the God we serve. I saw my daughter Amy grapple with this, but once her focus became her own obedience and not her husband's performance, Jesse changed on his own. Their marriage is ten years and three children strong today.

Yes, I know there are exceptions—some marriages must end—but I'm speaking of the casual attitude we take about our promises before God. None of us would ever come out and say, "It's all about me," but our actions can show it. We get brainwashed into thinking "I've spent myself on my family, and it's time for some personal fulfillment. Life is short, there has to be more. Maybe ballroom dancing . . ."

The mask of "I deserve more."

Like Barbara, my friend Allison Gappe Bottke spent her young womanhood as a radical feminist entrenched in the New Age movement. Molested and abused by a foster parent, she had given up on God long before she escaped the home at fifteen to get married. But her husband became her abuser, jailer, kidnapper, rapist, and attempted murderer. Hers is an amazing story. A mother at sixteen, divorced at eighteen, Allison reached her late twenties with an out-of-control rebel son.

Who wouldn't slip into guilt, self-blame, and hopelessness? "I blamed men for all my problems and raised the feminist banner higher," she told me.

After another marriage and divorce, several broken engagements, and multiple abortions, Allison's weight swelled. Feeling emotionally maimed, she found herself sitting in an evening church service hearing a pastor speak about being lost, having no direction and no hope. "I knew the sermon was meant for me.

"The next decade was my decade of discovery," she says. "Truth opened up to me as God healed the wounded child." Because our mess becomes our ministry, Allison has turned this testimony into a line of inspirational books called *God Allows U-turns.*

Talk about undisguised; Allison gives it to you straight. She urges women not to fall for the same deception. "Don't swallow the lines I did in my quest for happiness. Learn what God wants you to value. Let's go on the counterattack against the threats to our families."

Count me in.

Feminism began with a rallying cry: Value women more in society! Margaret Sanger, founder of the birth control movement said, "No woman can call herself free who does not own and control her own body. No woman can call herself free until she can choose consciously whether she will or will not be a mother."[3]

And it's still on the frontlines of the battle of ideas today.

Born into an Irish working-class family in 1879, Margaret saw her mother, a strong Catholic, die a slow death after eighteen pregnancies and eleven live births. It's not hard to see why Margaret thought pregnancy enslaved women. In those days, if you wanted to enjoy an amorous evening with your husband, you had to risk pregnancy.

Her goal to secure freedom for women was not wrong in itself, but it was her lack of biblical outlook that caused her to take it way too far. And as Barna says, "The reason people don't act like Jesus, is because they don't think like Jesus."[4]

To the nonbeliever God's ways seem as outdated as a typewriter. As Paul says, "People who aren't Christians can't understand these truths from God's Spirit" (1 Cor. 2:14 NLT). We can't expect them to, but we should know better.

Margaret started a radical magazine to promote feminism and argue for abortion. Her activism ruined her marriage, so to justify her views on sexual liberation she jumped into a series of affairs. Eventually she did remarry, but on her own terms. She insisted on financial and sexual independence.

Funny thing about self-expression, it can easily turn into self-deception and then self-destruction.

Susan B. Anthony, who ushered in the woman's right to vote, opposed abortion, not for reasons of faith but because it was unsafe. She blamed men and the laws they created for the "double standard" that drove women to abortion. Like many feminists of that era, she was certain that equality and freedom for women would end the need for abortion.

Modern society and its bent for "life on my terms" has proved her wrong.

You may have suffered the pain of abortion yourself. My daughter Amy has. During her wanderings, she made a decision based on what the world says is the easy way out. My shy daughter speaks out now, telling her story of how Christ shed light on how she was deceived, and how she found peace and forgiveness.

As the old commercial says, "We've come a long way, baby." We can now pursue careers in fields once open only to men, including military combat. We can take leadership positions in church, using our gifts, talents, and unique qualities to make a difference, but can't we leave our biblical womanhood intact too?

As a little girl, I was told to "mind your p's and q's" and "be a lady" because I was quite the tomboy, but my parents were talking about my behavior and the social niceties of the day. Nobody coached me on how to be fully a woman.

My early single years—as the breadwinner and Ms. Fix-it—stretched me, but toughened me too. As my red toolbox story highlights, the more self-sufficient I became, the less I needed men and the more I found fault with them.

Through healthy friendships with men who honored God, my attitude changed. I would always be plucky, outspoken, and opinionated—part of my natural sanguine personality—but I could be tender, open, and trusting, as well.

Xena, Warrior Princess

For once I agreed with the *Sacramento Bee* on a movie review about a remake of the old King Arthur tale a few years ago. The reviewer noted that Guinevere looked like she was auditioning for the next installment of *Xena, Warrior Princess*. "Guinevere wields a sword and dons an outrageously skimpy leather dominatrix outfit that looks as if it could have come out of Victoria's Secret's Halloween catalogue, circa A.D. 400. She also wears severe, foreboding war paint smeared on her face,"[5] the reviewer said.

On the radio the young actress insisted it was a thrill to play such a strong woman. She referred to her character as "a revisionist Guinevere." Whatever that means.

"There's a difference between a strong woman and a violent woman," the reviewer wrote. "Why is it that strong women on screen these days seem indistinguishable from men, exhibiting the same poor impulse control? We've reached a sad point when everything in movies has to be masculine, when it's considered weak—and uncommercial—to be soft and feminine."[6]

Amen to that. I have to wonder if Hollywood is out of touch or if this is what American women really want. Sexy bodies and strong muscles that can dislocate a guy's shoulder with a karate chop. Is that who we are supposed to be? Do women really want to work like men, play like men, and fight like men? It reminds me of Annie Oakley, a country tomboy and incredible riflewoman whose story is immortalized in *Annie Get Your Gun.* The play centers on her rivalry with Frank, the sharp shooting star of Buffalo Bill's Wild West Show. In one scene she sings: *"Anything you can do I can do better. . . . I can drink my liquor faster than a flicker, I can do it quicker and get even sicker."* Of course, Frank drops his pride and Annie gets the love of her life.

But competing with men is a dangerous game. It's not that we have to be *Stepford Wives,* turning into smiling, submissive robots; no—we were created to be confident and empowered for great things—but can't we enjoy being fully female?

And I don't mean wearing skirts (which I can't stand) and high heels (which I hate even more) or striving to look like a supermodel with a sleek body and cleavage. As a child I liked dolls well enough but my biggest thrills came from catching moths at midnight in the cage my father built, giant Polyphemos moths with fat bodies and feathery antennae. I'd study them for days. I loved preserving specimens in glass cases in my bedroom.

Not a very girlish thing to do.

By fully female, I mean to accept the way we are divinely created, develop our identity based on our uniqueness, and see ourselves as valuable to the kingdom of God, as Jesus did. Created not to compete with men, but to partner together with them as God leads. My author friend Kendry Smiley shared this to a group of women recently, and it spoke to every one of us. "Where is your identity? Is it in your purse or in your family or in your speaking or writing? Is it in your achievements or awards or titles or accolades? If it is, someone can steal it! If your identity is in the Lord, it can never be stolen."

I have to think of Esther again, a Jewess living as a Persian queen. The capital city hummed with ambassadors, scientists, and soldiers scurrying through the marketplace where thousands of Jews had small shops. The Jews, no longer in captivity, had been free to return to their Palestinian homeland for years, but why leave when Persian life was plush?

In Persia, liberalism reigned. You could worship your own gods and live by your national customs; nobody cared. The going philosophy was peaceful coexistence through tolerance.

Esther was steeped in this culture. *Do your own thing, but don't talk to us about your religion. We have dozens of gods of our own, and we like our lifestyle.* I have to wonder how many lukewarm Jews blended into the culture and drifted from their spiritual roots. When times are good, we tend to forget that we need God.

Our task today is similar to Esther's: to be God-fearing, God-loving women in a culture at odds with his truth when our neighbors and coworkers, even our relatives, are chasing material success, touting sexual freedom and declaring that morality is whatever you want it to be, depending on the situation.

I've had people tell me that Christians are narrow-minded. There's no room for tolerance and diversity. Christianity is so exclusionary.

America is a divided country. We're separated by moral issues such as the sanctity of marriage—we saw it in the 2004 elections—and I'm still hearing commentators debate about what exactly moral values are. Is morality a right-wing religious thing, or can we be fair minded and permissive—can we be pro-choice and pro-compromise for every lifestyle—and still have values?

We need to live out our faith according to God's word. As Christ followers we should be different from those who don't yet know him, to see the world through God's eyes, training ourselves to keep the Christian worldview. I go into this in depth in my book *Unshakeable: The Steadfast Heart of Obedience.* Christian worldview can be summed up in a single phrase: "Jesus is Lord." It's about embracing the truth of the

Creator and his claim on our lives. It's knowing what is expected of us as believers and living the God-ordered life without compromise.

According to George Barna only seven percent of those who call themselves Christians actually follow a Christian lifestyle. I'm still blown away by that, but I've seen it, smorgasbord Christianity—just pick and choose what parts of the Bible you want to accept. If it doesn't quite fit what you really want, disregard it. I've seen it with single women in what we call missionary dating. *It's okay if he's not a Christian. I've prayed about it and I know God's will is that I'm the one to bring him to the Lord. My situation is unique.* And yet the Bible is clear about not being mismatched (yoked) with unbelievers (2 Cor. 6:14). This isn't a suggestion, it's a command. *See, Christianity is exclusionary.*

If God says it, we can know it's for our benefit. But when our personal agenda—driven by our emotions—gets in the way, the blinders go on. Been there, done that. It's so easy to be fooled, to pray about a situation and "find" a Scripture that fits, claiming it's God's answer. It's selective perception. And it's our tendency to go to people for counsel when they'll tell us what we need to hear because "my situation is unique." Yet, if we looked deep enough we'd see that if we consulted God he would challenge us to look at it a different way.

No, forget that, because bottom line, we want what we want.

We live in a time of moral and philosophical confusion, and what threatens our faith today is this convenient Christianity. And without God's Word as a major prop in our production, we can lose our direction and wander into faulty thinking.

In a culture with a warped view of womanhood and a Christian community that's moving toward the entertainment-driven message and watered-down faith, we have to be on guard if we want to remain in the truth of who we are as woman who follow Jesus.

The Bible is the textbook on femininity, and I heard a speaker say once: Inventory your feminine character by the Word of God. "Nothing amazes God's woman. She is mentally and spiritually prepared for anything. She expects the unexpected and only goes to pieces for a moment or two. She is soft and strong."

This summer I saw Beth Moore speak in person for the first time. This girlish woman spoke with a power and authority clearly ordained by God. She wore a white skirt with ruffles trimmed in eyelet lace and a blue denim jacket. Denim and lace. What a great combination. Denim for strength, lace for femininity.

Creating women was God's idea. The world needs us and our perspective. "In the awe-inspiring generosity of the Lord," says Carolyn Mahaney, "we have been created with a unique task. If we cultivate and express our femininity with this in view, our Maker will commend us for the wise stewardship of this precious gift."[7]

Digging in Together

1. Take a look at 1 John 2:15–17. How are we most tempted to love the world? Read verse 20. Look up the word *anoint* in the dictionary and talk about what it means to us as we remain in God's truth.

2. It's a challenge to be a woman of God in today's world. Read Ruth 2:10–13; Proverbs 31:10; Ephesians 5:15; 6:10; and 1 Timothy 2:9 and discuss what biblical womanhood should look like in light of these passages.

3. Do you agree with the conclusion reached by Barna research that "Americans have fallen in love with faith rather than the object of their faith"? Have you seen evidence of this in your church or fellowship? See Philippians 3:7–8.

4. Take a look at Jesus' words to the disciples concerning the world in John 15:18–19. What are some practical ways we can be in the world but not of it?

Chapter 10

The Money Box

Money and wealth have the seductive power to take God's place.

A devout life does bring wealth, but it's the rich simplicity of being yourself before God. (1 Timothy 6:6 MSG)

As the new Persian queen, Esther lived in the land of silk and money. The palace at Susa, located near the present Iran-Iraq border, brimmed with magnificent treasures. Glazed brick walls, couches of gold and silver, mosaic pavement of marble and mother-of-pearl (Esther 1:6). Not exactly shabby chic.

Surrounded by opulence, Esther had unlimited access to pleasure. Frequent feasting and frolicking, the finest foods and wines—a far cry from an orphan's meager beginnings.

As the monarch's new wife, she was still the default queen, a replacement for the "rebellious" one. Not much security in that.

Our world measures our worth by the money we make and the way we display it. Money has the seductive power to take God's place, and we don't even know it—a lesson I learned the hard way.

As you know, before Carl proposed to me he explained his wish to leave the corporate world and start his own small one-man business, and was I okay with that? "Of course, follow your dream," I told him. Why not? I had a state job and a nice steady paycheck, so it never gave my heart an insecure stir. But after I found myself as a self-employed writer, we lived on what Carl dubbed "multiple pots of income."

And with crossed fingers I hoped they wouldn't spring any leaks.

"Don't worry, honey," he promised. "We'll make it." Where God guides, he provides, I told myself. Still I cut up my Nordstorm's credit card, started scoping out all the upscale thrift shops for designer clothes, and found the bag-your-own grocery store.

Hey, frugal can be fun.

Carl scouted around for opportunities to make some money to save for a rainy day. When he found a ramshackle house on a gorgeous wooded hilltop acre—that the bank would let go for a song—he said, "Let's renovate and resell it," *Sure, it's right up our creative alleys.* We signed the papers and rolled up our sleeves for a fun project together.

Six months later, an adorable cottage emerged and we put up the "for sale" sign, hoping to find a buyer. During the first hour of the open house a couple made an offer, and we made a deal. Recommitted Christians, they were looking for a fresh start in a new community. We extended our hands, hearts, and handiwork to them.

But two years later a process server knocked on our door with a summons. After he left I stood on the porch feeling as if I'd been shot with a stun gun. How could this be—a lawsuit over the adorable cottage? The accusing words could not be meant for us—fraud and negligence? We put our hearts into that property, and we tried to do everything top notch and right. Couldn't they have called us with a problem? What happened to working things out between friends? Court is not the answer for Christians.

The next eighteen months were torture—lawyers, depositions, and dread. And my first response was not to turn the other cheek. *See Jan clench her teeth.* We fixed everything visibly wrong, disclosed all known quirks, and resolved minor issues as they brought them up. But the old pipes finally burst in the kitchen—they accepted they were buying a forty-year-old house—and they discovered pockets of mold behind the walls.

Talk about an education! I learned there are thousands of types of mold, and it's found everywhere—indoors and out. Most are harmless, but some can cause illness in sensitive people. Experts ruled out the bad toxic mold. *No problem, let's just fix it then.* Replace the walls, the boards—whatever we need to do—and be done with it.

Not good enough for them. During that time there was a new wave of personal injury and mold lawsuits that were creating a public frenzy; plaintiffs were winning huge mold verdicts. I had some sleepless nights as the doom and gloom merchant paid me midnight visits. We are going to lose everything, I thought.

Grudge time for Jan; bitterness gripped me. It's one thing to be sued by nonbelievers, but people claiming to love Christ? Hate burned in me, but hating people is like burning down your own house to get rid of the rats. Wrong response.

Our insurance company attorney advised us to keep quiet for legal reasons. *What! I can't share my confusion, not even with my Friday morning prayer group?* Carl made me promise not to breathe a word. Talk about misery and migraines. They came back with vengeance.

I'll just hire a first-rate lawyer who's never lost a case and fight this thing, I thought. But that wouldn't happen unless we had $150,000 lying around for a defense fund. The insurance company had their limits—in California they refuse to cover mold claims at all anymore because of all the irresponsible lawsuits. Bottom line: there were no federal or state standards at that time for this problem, a new issue for California courts. Few precedents had been set for such disputes.

We were advised to settle the case through mediation. I must tell you it felt like being interrogated as a foreign spy or something.

"They want what?" I screamed when we learned of their demands. "But that's four times more than they paid for the property! And the problems are all fixable. How can they be pressing for so much more?"

"Emotional pain and suffering" and a host of other senseless demands that the lawyer rattled off with a shrug. Twelve hours later we settled, and while our insurance company kicked in their absolute maximum, we were obligated to pay a five-figure chunk of money that we would borrow against our home equity.

"Not fair," I cried driving home. The next morning I woke up to mall hunger, the urge to go shopping, pamper myself with some new clothes, anything to splurge and spend. After it passed, I ranted at God. *Just think of the ministries we could have supported with this money!* Then, silently at Carl. *It's all your fault.* Next, at the plaintiffs—well, let's forget what I muttered about them after I heard that they bulldozed the cottage and built a big new house with the money they won from us.

Misery needs strong black tea, so I fetched my favorite china cup from the hutch, filled it with steaming English Breakfast, and slid into my burgundy recliner. *Lord, this is such a waste. What is the purpose? Help me see it through your eyes.*

Epiphany time for Jan.

Cobwebs from the Past

My mother's heart may have been closed, but Daddy's checkbook was always open to his daughter if she really *needed* it. My parents weren't rich, but they worked hard and invested well. And somehow I grew up believing that being loved meant being taken care of financially. Then my first husband bounced from job to job, searching for his place in the professional world. He encouraged me to be a stay-at-home mom, and I had no control over our shaky income. Once single, the fear of being homeless swamped me, but Dad stepped in. He footed the bill for my attorney, helped me get on my feet until my first paycheck, and paid for an expensive teen recovery program for my wayward daughter Amy.

If our feelings toward God are a picture of our youth, it's no wonder money meant a safety net to me. Money would keep the wolves from the door, and like Scarlett O'Hara clutching the red dirt of Tara in *Gone with the Wind,* I vowed after my divorce to "never be hungry again."

The lawsuit uncovered my "lover of money" mask, the one I denied owning. After all, anyone can tell you Jan is a cheerful giver. When I finally began making a good salary at the State Capitol, I was generous Jan. And I always took my young teen daughters on marathon shopping sprees for fun, or so I thought.

We know that once you search for truth you find it, and it was not hard to see that behind those shopping trips were guilt and the hope to win their affections. And how many times had spending been my first response to stress, the hope that buying could somehow bring soothing? Depression shopping, I called it.

Until I came face to face with this truth, I scoffed at my daughters when each said separately, "Money is power to you, Mom."

I flinched at the sound of that. Could there be truth in it? And money had begun to strain my marriage to Carl. He felt the pressure to provide for me like my father, who saved and sacrificed for his daughter's future.

His spoiled daughter.

Carl blamed himself for the lawsuit—he'd made a bad call and let me down. He knew I blamed him, too, though I never voiced it. Resentment sizzled below the smile, and I had the strong desire to take control of the bank books, give up writing, and go back to a real job with real money. Is this what Scripture means, I wondered, that the love of money is the root of all kinds of evil? But, I don't *love* money, that's not it. It's because extra money can help others, further the kingdom of God. Right?

Yes, but I got off kilter. This was me: "Some people, eager for money, have wandered from the faith and pierced themselves with many griefs" (1 Tim. 6:10).

Pierced? How about skewered? Finally, it made sense. *Your security is still in what you own, in your investments,* I concluded with a grimace. *Look at your response to this lawsuit. It's out of balance. Possessions cannot protect you from harm or assure you a future. They are fleeting, just hay and stubble. Your security must be in God alone.*

Who was my true provider? If the God of the universe allowed this lawsuit then it must be for a reason, and the ultimate outcome—whatever the cost—is for my own good, to build my character, to make me more effective for him.

Wow. Revelation time.

The following weekend I spoke on "The Fragrant Journey," a theme chosen by the retreat team. They asked me if I would lead the women in a time of surrender after my session on Saturday night. I chuckled at God's timing. Lead them in surrender? *Well, Jan, you'll be speaking to yourself this weekend, about letting go of spiritual hindrances and being a sweet aroma of Christ.* So I invited the ladies to jot down their burdens, what they wanted to let go of, and tuck the papers inside small octagon-shaped boxes of gold, wrapped in purple ribbon. Next, each lady would leave her box on the altar to signify giving up, letting go.

I followed suit, scribbling "financial security, my unhealthy hold on money." What an unforgettable night for me. The little box now sits on my dresser, and whenever I get a twinge of anxiety about the future, I remember what I promised to yield to God.

Surrender raises the curtain on the right perspective. Suddenly I saw it from God's view. If an unfair lawsuit helped liberate me from something that weighted me down, then I can be thankful for it.

Not to mention the privilege of flexing my mercy muscle while praying for the plaintiffs, a stretch at first. But I returned to what I know: process the feelings, own them all—every last ugly one—then find the way to forgiveness. That's the way it works with me.

Money is such a deceiver. We think we need it for happiness, that it can solve our problems and protect us against disaster. Make money your god, they say, and it will plague you like the Devil. Someone once asked Andrew Carnegie, who made a fortune in steel, "How much is enough?" And he said, "Just a little more."

The people who sued us are still in litigation, four years later, with their own insurance company. I guess they need just a little more.

For money, some will sell their soul. Remember the motive behind Judas betraying Jesus? Money. And look at Delilah, motivated by greed. For a reward from the rich and powerful rulers in Philistine, she went to work on Samson the mighty warrior and used her charms to strip him of his strength. The lure of money always tests our integrity. Delilah valued cash more than relationship (Judg. 16).

A few years ago our church hosted a one night mini-seminar on how to become debt free. Hundreds of people jammed our sanctuary to hear strategies for paying off credit cards and tips to establish a budget plan. Two evenings later came our monthly "Refresh and Refuel." When you enter the dim-lit room to soft praise songs and fragrant candles, you can spend time at any of the assorted prayer stations; there's even a hammer if you want to nail up some burdens as you release them to the Lord.

Only nine people showed up for that.

The numbers spoke volumes to me about how we're caught in the money maze. And I've been there. The speaker that night, a financial planner, said something profound: If more people would pay as they go, they might catch up paying for where they've already been. Ouch. You might be squirming right now and saying, "She has no idea what it takes to keep my head above water." And you're right, I don't know your story, nor will I offer any budget tips because everybody's situation is different. I can only share how I placed too much faith in the god of money. And it may tempt me the rest of my life.

There's not a thing wrong with enjoying the fruits of your labors and surrounding yourself with comforts and having fun. I'm in the redecorating stage right now, and am having a blast shopping for new accessories to spice up my house. And Carl and I love to travel.

My husband sold his small business and became a "real estate consultant" as he calls it. He is gifted at helping people. Right now, our multiple pots of income are running over, but we know it won't last forever, and that's okay. I am trying to keep it in perspective so money won't deceive or control me again. And for Carl it's a double challenge. He comes back from touring somebody's gorgeous dream home with a view of the Sierras and has to adjust his contentment barometer. His industry is filled with movers and shakers and money seekers.

But we know that money could lead us astray, because it's a pursuit that tempts us to depend on things instead of God.

Wealth will never define our worth, and worldly pleasures can be empty indulgences. Instead, we want to indulge ourselves in God now. "Turn my eyes away from worthless things; preserve my life according to your word" (Ps. 119:37).

Sure, we should enjoy the present and save for the future, but God challenges us to think beyond material goals and to keep money in perspective. His goal has never been our comfort, but our character. And he'll stop at nothing to make us more like Christ, even a financial crisis. It helps me to remember that God is more intent on making us holy than happy, and nothing of his is accessible through my checkbook.

Digging in Together

1. How difficult is it for you to treat money and material possessions as if they belong to God? See Mark 10:21–23 and Matthew 6:24.

2. What are some of the traps set by today's world that we fall into

when it comes to material wealth? Read Luke 12:15–21. What are some ways to avoid the traps?

3. Read Luke 16:10–13. According to these verses, struggling with money issues was a common problem even in Bible times. Has a money issue ever tested your integrity or faith?

4. Think about the way you live and how you spend your money. What could you live without and still be content?

5. Read 1 Timothy 6:9–10. Have you known someone who has chased money and wandered from the faith?

Act 3

Moving Beyond the Facade

Act 3 is the Act of Resolution. Everything has built up to the climax, where our leading lady has no more need to struggle. Her dilemma, introduced at the onset of our story, is resolved. We've watched her wrestle with her dark side, own her experiences, embrace her backstory. We've seen her move toward shedding her prideful spirit, squashing her faulty logic, and letting go of her desperate need to control. She's died to many of her fantasies and unrealistic expectations.

She has achieved what she's always wanted. The light of truth has come on. She discovers the hidden part of herself, the woman behind the mask.

She's moving beyond convenient Christianity, preferring to speak and walk in the truth.

Everything, all the action and emotional turmoil, has led up to this point, and we hear her speak, "It's all been worth it."

The curtain comes down and the audience heads for the door, smiling. The main tension is gone. The fear that our leading lady would bail out and give up has vanished.

The play was a smash because we identify so much with her, and we leave with our heart full of hope.

Chapter 11

The Understudy:
A Most Important Role

The best actors are those who are willing to learn their craft.

I am the LORD your God, who teaches you what is best for you, who directs you in the way you should go. (Isaiah 48:17)

If you've ever watched *Oklahoma,* you may remember the irrepressible Ado Annie, the girl who can't stop flirting. She's the comic relief in the musical, and if there was ever a part made for me, this had to be it. So I immersed and rehearsed and came prepared for the high school audition. I looked the director in the eye and managed not to fall apart, and I've never belted out a more perfect song:

> I can't be prissy or quaint.
> I ain't the type that can't faint.
> How can I be what I ain't?
> I can't say . . . no.

To my shock the role went to another, but I donned my mask of "I didn't want it that bad anyway." And then I was asked if I might consider the role of understudy. *Here we go again, always second best.* All that work, preparing like crazy for the moment that may never come, secretly wanting to poison the real Annie.

No thanks. I turned it down.

What a dummy. Anyone in the theater will tell you that while the understudy may be the hardest job, it brings the greatest opportunity. Being invisible becomes a blessing in disguise. You are there "just in case," to fill in so the show can go on, and you must be familiar with the entire production. Being an understudy forces you to observe all the nuances and finer points of the role, listen intently and learn much.

At the time, my wounded child said "thumbs down" to accepting the role of understudy, unaware of how character-building it would be. My immaturity demanded that it take center stage or nothing at all.

Proverbs says we should apply our hearts to instruction and our ears to words of knowledge (23:12). Teachability is another word for willingness. To learn from those that God places in our lives, especially authentic women who are living a life of integrity. As their understudies, we can profit from their wisdom and learn from their mistakes. But most of us are, I'm afraid, addicted to being the star of our own show and forget not only how to ask for words of wisdom but how to train our ears to hear them.

At one point in my legislative career, I hired all the support staff for the office. New at this I asked a friend and former supervisor for some advice. "Never be impressed by fancy resumes," she told me. "Get a feel for whether or not your candidate has a teachable spirit. Be less concerned about skills and more about willingness."

This is advice that will never prove wrong.

Solomon said, "Cry out for insight and understanding. Search for them as you would for lost money or hidden treasure. Then you will understand what it means to fear the Lord, and you will gain knowledge of God" (Prov. 2:3–5 NLT).

Scripture has much to say about wisdom: It is more valuable than gold (Prov.16:16), and true wisdom demands humility, an admission that we just don't have all the answers. We can drop our mask and ask for advice, consider other viewpoints. We can borrow an attitude from what Albert Einstein once said, the more I know, the more I realize I don't know.

A few years back at our church's women's retreat—I went as a participant not the speaker—I saw Diana pacing the floor with her infant boy in a cozy sling across her chest. Because I love babies, I stopped to make a fuss over him. "Jan, you're an older woman," Diana said. "Maybe I can get your counsel on something." Then her eyes grew wide. "I didn't mean older that way—oh, did I say that?"

"It's all right, Diana. I'm honored." Yes, I am one of those *older* women Paul mentions—and he meant more mature in Christ, not years—that "must train the younger women to love their husbands and their children, to live wisely and be pure, to take care of their homes, to do good, and to be submissive to their husbands" (Titus 2:4–5 NLT). And as Proverbs says, teach them the ropes and give them a grasp on reality (Prov. 1:4 MSG).

Diana ignored the women arriving and brushing past us to the registration table. "I've got to tell you," she said. "I'm having a difficult time." Her husband had just announced his desire to go into full-time ministry. "And I'm bucking it big time."

No wonder. As a preacher's kid, Diana spent her youth riding the roller coaster of rebellion, and later searched for love in all the wrong places. When we first met, she sang in our choir and was raising a young daughter from an early relationship. When Bob, handsome, thirty-something, and still single, arrived at church eager to serve the Lord, it was instant and mutual attraction. One day I cautioned her to *take it slow,* advice she ignored. But once married I saw her change and grow, evidenced by her willingness to be real in expressing her frustration to me, asking for advice this time.

Diana had waited a lifetime for Mr. Right, but *no way* did she want to be a pastor's wife after growing up as a pastor's daughter. *Forget it.* "How did this happen?" she wondered. Why didn't he tell her this before? Because he simply hadn't known it at the time, not until he got involved in ministry and found his passion.

The night we spoke Diana was in the panic stage, and she just needed a reality check, that if God called Bob into ministry, he'd prepare her for it and it would not be the end of the world. Asking for counsel revealed Diana's maturity in seeking a wise word from another woman.

The same week my daughter Amy called to run a marriage question by me. What a contrast to the girl who couldn't wait to do the opposite of anything Mom ever recommended. I had a few suggestions, and she phoned later to say, "It worked. You are so wise, Mom." You should see the big happy face I drew on my notepad.

Not all of us have a mother we can turn to, but teaching can come from any mentor in your life. Since Amy has been without a father since age fourteen, she asks Carl's take on things quite often, and she actually heeds some of his counsel, not all, but still, I'm quite impressed.

My friend Roanne never bonded with her divorced and troubled mother, but God provided a precious grandmother as a spiritual north star. "Nana taught me there is a God. A picture of Jesus always sat reverently on her piano. If something was going on in my life, she got down on her hands and knees and talked to God about it. Early on I realized the truth in her values and aimed to be just like Nana, giving out what she gave me—love, faith, patience, loyalty, and unconditional acceptance."

My Grandma Hallie was my guiding star, and now that I'm "older" in the Lord I want to pass on to younger women what God has taught me. We can't inherit wisdom, but we can apply truth and discover it. Asking where others have walked can give us enough light for an uncertain path.

The S Words: Submission and Surrender

Lisa Paparraro is the founder of W.I.S.E.—Women In Search of Excellence—and teaches weekly Bible studies in our community, mentoring many area women in their search for knowledge of God. One Sunday she gave the morning message . . . on submission. A word guaranteed to bring sneers. Giving up. Giving in. Mouse. Doormat. Coward.

We see it as a dirty word, but are we ever wrong. Sorry, but I can't discuss the teachable spirit without talking about the *s* word.

When the Bible instructs us to submit to our husbands, that they are the head of the home (Eph. 5:22–23), it's a hard concept for modern Christian woman to grasp. Lisa runs across this frequently in her ministry, and sees two responses: (1) I am woman—hear me roar, and (2) Let him make all the decisions; I'll just abdicate.

Two extremes, and both are way out of balance.

"The enemy is trying to trip us up," she told us. "We have the mistaken idea that the person in the submitted role is less valuable, but it is a role, a position. Christ's submission to God was not based on passivity or weakness."

Shortly after I became a Christian, my soon-to-be ex-husband came by the house to get something and looked at me with one eyebrow raised. "You've changed. You're so different. This house is so . . . peaceful." You could just see his yearning for the peace that passes all understanding, the peace only Christ can give. He was struggling with his decision to sever from our family, and I was certain God would draw him home. If I could just keep it up—my peaceful spirit—my white picket fence future might happen after all.

He must like me better this way, I thought, devout and demure. So that's the mask I decided to wear.

In our faith beginnings, we can get confused about what the authentic Christian woman looks like. In her book *The Myth of the Submissive Christian Woman,* Brenda Waggoner describes it as disappearing behind the mask of what we think our new spiritual identity should be, desperate to "die to self." "I lived a lot of years by the name Princess Hides Herself," Brenda says in her book. "From around age twelve until I was forty-something, that name described how I lived because I thought that was what it meant to die to self and let Christ live inside of me. The freedom of Spirit that Jesus talked about eluded me, although I wouldn't admit it."[1]

You might have grown up like Brenda and me, with this same misperception, that we had to conceal our true nature for some reason. When I found Christ, I soon adopted the idea that the zany side of me—the entertainer—must be held in check because it's not what spiritual women should do. Yesterday I bumped into an old friend from church whose husband sought deeper teaching, so they're now in a small fellowship in a nearby town. He's happy, but she's struggling to find her place there. "Jan," she confessed. "I feel like I have to tone down my dress to come to church. These women are so conservative, so saint-like, they home school their children. They are the traditional woman, and I've always been out in the world with a career. I love these gals, but feel like I have to soft pedal who I really am."

Where did we get this submissive woman thing so messed up? That it's somehow about our demeanor and not about simply having a yielded heart? It doesn't mean ignoring your own needs or serving everyone else constantly or letting others make choices for you. It's wanting Christ's righteousness more than anything.

Susan, the women's ministry director who asked me to speak on "The Fragrant Journey" theme has become an e-mail friend. I let her know about my latest book, and she shared with me her struggles. Abused as a child, Susan turned to food; it became her best friend, and after a disastrous divorce, she ran to it for comfort. She sampled the smorgasbord of weight loss plans with only temporary success, and finally she gave in. "My weight is bondage from the enemy, one of the most consuming areas of my life."

One of her journal entries reveals her transparency with this struggle: "Father, here I am again. Another Monday morning, another weekend of failure, another time of disgust and self-loathing because I have once again surrendered to food instead of you. Lord, I love you with all my heart; or so I profess. But I continue to turn to food for so many reasons: loneliness, frustration, celebration, comfort. God, I know that whenever I eat when I'm not truly hungry, I am attempting to fill an emptiness that only you can touch. Lord, please forgive me."

Oswald Chambers said that the weakest saint can experience the power of the Son of God once she is willing to let go. We have to keep letting go, and slowly but surely the great full life of God will invade us in every part.[2] When we come to the place of complete abandonment, God can use us. "God revealed to me that the freedom is there," Susan said. "It has already been bought at the cross, but it can only become a reality through my surrender."

Surrender of the control of our lives is the Christian message—obedience to his will, loving him enough to give our future to him.

When we come to the place where our relationship with our King means more than anything else on our list—a relationship, a promotion, more money—wisdom appears. It takes effort to tap into it and patience to profit by it.

Wisdom is supreme says Solomon, therefore get it though it cost all you have (Prov. 4:7). Wisdom is the tree of life (Prov. 3:18). The Queen of Sheba traveled twelve hundred miles to talk with King Solomon. "Solomon answered all her questions; nothing was too hard for the king to explain to her" (1 Kings 10:3). And the king gave the queen "all she desired and asked for, besides what he had given her out of his royal bounty" (1 Kings 10:13).

You don't have to take a road trip to find wisdom. It may only be a phone call or a ride across town to ask a godly woman's counsel. Take notice and never be too proud or too stubborn to be an understudy. Though you may watch the show night after night from behind the curtain, almost invisible, you live constantly in the moment, alert, yet so relaxed and free. You're content in your role, because it's not about you being the star, but you being available. And you are ready for that last minute call should it come, "We need you now." And when it does, you see that all your training and experience is for this moment, this call to action. And despite your opening night jitters, you will rise to the occasion. Yes, it's "baptism by fire," but this is God's stage, and this is how he works.

And when the curtain comes up and you step out, you are willing to give it your best, because the show must go on.

Digging in Together

1. Read Proverbs 6:20–23. Share a time when you received advice from a parent or elder and disregarded it. Were there any recognizable consequences?
2. Proverbs 11:14 and 15:22 say to seek counsel from those with experience and godly wisdom. Who are your best advisors? Describe their experience and godly wisdom. Share something valuable you learned from a mentor in your life.
3. Read Isaiah 47:13. Have you ever sought advice from several people, only to be confused with the assorted answers?
4. The wise woman is always a student, eager to learn the ways of God. What are some of the barriers to a teachable spirit?
5. What are the benefits of true wisdom, and how should it form our character? See James 3:17–18.

Chapter 12

Balancing Act

Balance comes when we stop striving to *do* and let God teach us to *be*.

May your whole spirit, soul and body be kept blameless at the coming of our Lord Jesus Christ. (1 Thessalonians 5:23)

One of my favorite musicals is *The Unsinkable Molly Brown,* the true but trumped-up tale of spunky Margaret Tobin, the daughter of a penniless Irish immigrant who strikes out to seek her fortune on the Colorado gold fields. Before she leaves the Missouri log cabin, her Pa gives Maggie this advice: "Learn to serve God and a big breakfast."

Odd advice wouldn't you say, but solid counsel for a young woman—or any woman—searching for her place in the world. *Make sure you balance the spiritual and the practical.*

Learn to serve God. Okay, we'll get more into that later. God wants to use us if we're willing. And he does his best work at the grass roots level. He'll use us right where we are. And as Mother Teresa said, "We can do no great things—only small things with great love."[1] Learning to serve God begins by reaching out in authenticity to another woman and inviting her on a journey to wholeness with Christ.

But "serve a big breakfast," what does that mean? Chewing on this I came up with an answer. We all know that breakfast is the most important meal of the day. Skip it and you get light-headed—at least

I do—and your thinking gets fuzzy. A hearty breakfast boosts the metabolism, levels the blood sugar, and sets the tone for the day. Plus, if you cook a big breakfast, there's always enough to share with unexpected company.

Pa was telling Maggie, "Daughter, you're leaving the nest, starting out on your own. You best know this—get your priorities right. It's all about balance."

The story of *Unsinkable Molly Brown* is a fun movie to watch, but much of it is pure Hollywood bunk. She was never called Molly, she never worked as a barmaid or burned up the first million in the wood stove. Once she married J. J. Brown and they struck gold, she enjoyed being rich and made no excuses for it. She loved extravagant clothes and outlandish jewelry, and while she hoped for acceptance into Denver society, making the social register did not consume her.

But, did she learn to serve God and a big breakfast? I like to think so.

Wealth landed in Maggie's lap, and she used it to serve others. She set up soup kitchens for the poor and spearheaded the building of a new church. She had a heart as rich as her bank account. By the time Maggie Brown sailed on the fated ship *Titanic*—and saved fourteen women from freezing in the icy Atlantic—she had already made a huge impact on her little world. History books call her an "American original"—"the first to use her fabulous wealth not to mimic the Old World but to be flamboyantly, confidently herself."[2]

The fourth judge of Israel—and the only woman, by the way—was Deborah, the prophetess of Judges who ruled the nation and held court to mediate the people's disputes. When she told Barak that the Lord wanted him to take ten thousand men into battle, he refused to go without Deborah, though we're not told why. She agreed to go, and knowing the men would follow him into battle, she let him take the lead; but it was Deborah who planned and directed the entire campaign. A powerful leader, she knew her strengths and acted on them. She was also a wife who had a heart to serve God, a good balance, and I would say a woman *confidently herself.*

Like Esther. I picture her as a woman who is beautiful, but doesn't try and impress you with her appearance. She had knowledge, but didn't fling it around. She could hold her own in a conversation but keep quiet when necessary. She was confident, but not forceful. She had a gracious charm that included making others feel valued.

Though different personalities, Maggie, Deborah, and Esther were women of balance.

Going Solo

Esther had no real intimacy with the man she married; he was her bedmate, but not her soul mate, at least not during the writing of the book. She lived spiritually single. I hear of this heartbreak often. This is how Meg* describes it in an e-mail: "I am married to an unbeliever. My husband doesn't stand in my way of worshiping God, but he doesn't want any part of it, which excludes him from the part of me that is really me."

Meg longs to share the essence of who she really is—spirit as well as body—with her husband. A familiar story, and one in which you may find yourself or a dear friend. I've seen this scenario many times and can offer you this encouragement: things change when we take our focus off changing our spouse and instead are open to God changing us. I know it's easier said than done. Again I think of Esther who had little influence over King Xerxes, not his decisions at court or his extramarital flings. But later, we see his heart soften. I like to think he became a believer in the Hebrew God after Esther's courage saved her people.

I'm learning that patience is vital in all relationships, but especially with unbelieving spouses. They don't see things the way we do. Think back before you knew the Lord and how distorted your vision was. Trust God's purpose in your marriage even if you can't see it right now. Many women I speak with bring up the blessings they are receiving as they walk in obedience with the Lord in their marriage. Be your own person, don't hide your light.

In the early years of my singleness, a verse from Isaiah brought me comfort and helped me remember that my primary role was to please God, whether I ever married or not. The true intimacy I sought would come from my relationship with him. I posted this on my fridge: "For your Maker is your husband—the LORD Almighty is his name—the Holy One of Israel is your Redeemer; he is called the God of all the earth" (Isa. 54:5).

Solomon discovered the secret to harmony in life: understanding God's timing. Before I ever heard of the book of Ecclesiastes, the Byrds were crooning *Turn! Turn! Turn!* on the radio. The 1965 hit song made a comeback in the movie *Forrest Gump*. It was biblically inspired. *There is a time for everything, and a season for everything under heaven.* To be born, die, plant, uproot, tear down, build up, mourn, dance. I heard the song on my favorite oldies station the other day. It has a spiritual meaning to me now. We need to enter each new season of life, *turn* into it with expectation.

God is a God of seasons, and each one has its purpose.

I turned into my single season with dread, as if I were a captive Jew bound hand and foot by the Babylonians, carried kicking and screaming into exile. Not a thing to look forward to except the long and boring desert with no oasis in sight. I was certain that I'd have to live the rest of my life in the penalty box, off to the side of the ice-hockey rink where the players wait for permission to skate again . . . after they've messed up in front everybody.

I was too green to understand about God's timing and how he coaches us in the dark for our debut under the lights. I had no clue how God would use the season of singleness for my good, to revamp my mind and soul. (He forgot about my body, but I've forgiven him for that.)

During this season I discovered my talents and gifts, and that I could use them in ministry. If I had known what was ahead—all the growth spurts and the wisdom to be gleaned—would I have resisted this season?

No way. Imagine my surprise to find myself content after a few years of going solo. The quarantine lifted. I no longer felt detained by my unfortunate situation, but discharged to go out and serve a gracious God, so thankful for my unwelcome season. He had given me a role to play in this season, as a leader of a singles ministry in town. I wrote skits and planned mixer games, and I gave our team my needed unique perspective. The season turned out to be more enjoyable than I imagined—and to think I almost turned it down.

My daughter Amy has three young children. Recently she shared this: "Mom, I love them, but every day is the same thing. I get up and do it all over again. And it's such tedious work." I can recall those endless days of crying babies, strong-willed preschoolers, jam smeared on the wall, the toilet plugged up with toys, and the never-ending house-hold chores.

It's a tough road for Amy right now. Money is tight, the house is small and chaotic, and she sometimes feels trapped by her choice to stay home. Yet, it's a major production just to leave the house for errands. She can't seem to manage a weekly Bible study or fellowship group, though she longs for the sisterly support. Still, she knows, "I need to make the most of this time with my kids and enjoy this season. It will go by so quickly."

Boy, does it. *My little girl has three kids now?*

Accepting our seasons is about adjusting to change, and change is an inevitable part of life in every generation, and we the women are usually the ones who make it work.

Mobile Living

I think of Priscilla from Acts 18. Talk about transition. When we meet her she is an exile from Rome living in a movable tent with hubby Aquila. When the apostle Paul arrives in Greece, he is welcomed into their humble shelter, and not only that, they offer to share their tent-making business with him too.

Imagine being forced to leave your home and wander the roads carting your house with you. And we're not talking any luxury RV either. Four flaps and a dirt floor, but Priscilla made the best of it. She couldn't change the facts—the old life was gone—but she could alter the future by changing the way she looked at it. And she became a partner to her husband in God's work. She used her gift of hospitality and opened her mobile home to seekers of the truth. And you don't see Priscilla just buttering bagels in the background; she is her husband's professional and spiritual equal. Together they educated young believers about Christ and the Holy Spirit.

When Paul leaves Corinth and sails for Syria, Priscilla and Aquila pull up tent stakes and go along. Whenever Paul mentions the couple—in Acts, Romans, 1 Corinthians—note that Priscilla's name always comes first. An interesting fact to share with those who think Christianity is sexist and promotes the idea that women are inferior. "Greet Priscilla and Aquila," he told the Romans. "They have been co-workers in my ministry for Christ Jesus. In fact, they risked their lives for me" (Rom. 16:3–4 NLT).

It helps me to look at change as an opportunity, but to risk your life for it? Yikes, I hope God never asks me, but if he did it would require digging up a spirit of willingness, like we talked about in the last chapter. Priscilla played a starring role in early Christian history, and she could only do it by living intentionally and unencumbered. The mobile home was a blessing in disguise for what God had planned for her.

Adapting to change depends on our attitude and outlook. One of my pet phrases is a lost beatitude I picked up somewhere: *Blessed are the flexible, for they shall not be bent out of shape.* I think of missionary wives and what it must be like as they partner with their husbands, accept different assignments, travel, pack, and unpack every few years.

We're always in transition, always growing and changing in some way. Every new season of our lives is a new frontier, a time of exodus, leaving the Red Sea of security behind for the unknown. It's deciding what to keep for each journey and what to leave behind. About finding new ways to build relationships and keep in touch with old ones. It's about developing new routines and learning to be flexible.

Oh, don't we fear change? We worry about what life will be like on the new frontier. And there's always a sense of loss for the old ways that are slipping away. Whether it's getting married, moving the family out of state, sending the last child to school, turning forty, reentering the workforce, or beginning a blended family; the old comfortable life is lost—we have to grieve for it—and we struggle to adapt to the new.

Think of all the scriptural good-byes to the old life: Rebecca, Sarah, Ruth, and Priscilla left their homeland for new adventures with no idea of the outcome or how God would ready them for his purpose.

It takes flexibility to adapt to a changing world, and we can all use a megadose of it.

Many of us juggle a home, career, family, and church, not to mention community service too. If you're a working mother you're facing the where-to-find-good-daycare dilemma and how to meet all the needs of your family. As a single-again you've got the complexities of divorce and child-sharing. As a wife, you have your husband's career and working around his needs. For some it's the stress of caring for an aging parent on top of it. For the young single woman, there's the challenge of career choices, pressures to find the love of your life, how to maintain healthy friendships with men, the whole dating dilemma and how to stay pure. And in a society rampant with divorce, the fear of being another statistic.

How do we balance the load? I have no pat answers, and as you know lists and tips are not my strength. If I've learned anything it's stick with my strengths, so, for me to share some strategies for the balanced life, I'd have to borrow them from somebody else.

Take Care of Your Inner Life

As my friend Joanna Weaver highlights in her book, *Having a Mary Heart in a Martha World,* the need for balance is every woman's tale. "Deep inside of you there is a hunger, a calling, to know and love God. To truly know Christ and the fellowship of the Spirit. You're not after more head knowledge—it's heart-to-heart intimacy you long for. Yet part of you hangs back. Exhausted, you wonder how to find the strength or time. Nurturing your spiritual life seems like one more duty—one more thing to add to a life that is spilling over with responsibilities."[3]

Eugenia Price, a favorite author of historical sagas, spent her first thirty-three years with a heavy heart. Sixty pounds overweight, she was deep in debt and lying to her creditors. Filled with resentment, blame, and self-disgust for digging such a deep hole, she avoided the truth. "I just kept dodging it and declaring more loudly that I loved things as they were!" she wrote in her autobiography, *The Burden Is Light.*[4]

I'm okay. It's fine. The performing took its toll. Eugenia's life was a burden, "and I was tired from carrying it myself. Tired, bored, and afraid to admit I was afraid." It made no sense; she had a nice house, friends she loved, and a good job. Why was everything so out of balance?

It was her chaotic, self-centered inner life. Once she surrendered to Christ, another Eugenia emerged. The masks came off as "my Creator called me back to the natural, into the joy of oneness with him. I was free of having to *be* somebody now."[5]

That's the first act of a balanced life. To stop our frantic scurrying around and pause for a God break. We make the mistake of trying to change our routines and habits, plan new approaches to our chaos, and call it balance. Nope, just a temporary fix. Lasting change springs from the mind and heart, not the day planner.

It's easy to think that balance will magically appear when I can rearrange my life, when the big project is done at work or when the kids are back in school. When I can just get a housekeeper twice a month—that's my banter.

It's easy to miss the point. Learning to serve God and a big breakfast is about rearranging your life around God's purposes. Everything else will find its place. The externals—the job, relationships, duties, and responsibilities—are the props in the drama of your life.

You take care of your inner life and let God rearrange the props.

Teresa of Avila's deep spiritual hunger led her to enter a Carmelite convent in Spain in 1535, but it was far from what she expected. Eager to leave, a mystery illness kept her stuck in the situation for three more years. Through this "thorn in her side" Teresa began what she described as "recollective prayer"[6]—what our church calls worship-based prayer. Not asking God for anything, but simply seeking him in worship and praise.

Soon she felt fully alive and understood what a balanced life meant.

If only she could teach what she had learned to others, so she kept lobbying Rome until they gave her a convent of her own. It was not even close to the traditional. Music and dancing were a big part of the day. "Just because the order is austere, there is no need for austere people," she said. "Virtue and merriment go hand in hand."[7]

Honor and joy are divinely linked. As are prayer and action, she claimed. She discovered decades ago what we need to relearn now; the busy life is fruitless without prayer and worship, and it must be balanced with fun and spontaneity.

Smart girl, this nun. I like her.

Teresa's approach started a reform movement that swept through Spain. Four centuries later, the Catholic Church made her saint.

Then there's Lydia from the book of Acts, a woman with both sandaled feet on the ground. A sharp businesswoman, Lydia didn't let her career goals affect her faith or commitment to family. Her story opens as she's gathered with some women friends outside Philippi. When Paul speaks, the Lord opens her heart.

Lydia leaves her coffee klatch—or board of directors meeting, whatever it was—and hurries home to share the good news with her family to make sure, the Bible says, the whole household was baptized. Bringing the Good News to her loved ones took priority.

Then she urges Paul to take a room at her house and continue preaching in the community. *My business can wait, God's work is more important.* Lydia's hospitality helped Paul's ministry expand far into the region. Lydia had literally learned to serve a big breakfast as she fed the endless stream of guests who gathered in her kitchen to hear about Jesus.

Strive for simplicity. Be strong yet gentle, express your feminine side while you strive in the marketplace. Dwell in the now and be flexible when God moves you. Be real. Build your house on a rock but design it with a bay window into your soul.

Digging in Together

1. See Proverbs 14:1. How do activities become stumbling blocks?
2. How would you describe your inner life: chaotic and self-centered like Eugenia Price, steady and balanced like Esther, or somewhere in between?
3. Read Hebrews 11:8–10. Sarah followed her husband, Abraham, to a new home. When you're in transition, what should be your focus?
4. Ecclesiastes 3:1–8 is Solomon's famous "time for everything" list. If we see these as seasons, what does it say about balance in our lives?
5. Where is your eye of the tornado, the place where you discern God's voice amidst the distractions?

Chapter 13

Supporting Players

Friends inspire and enrich our lives.

*The heartfelt counsel of a friend is as sweet as perfume and incense.
(Proverbs 27:9 NLT)*

I met my best friend in a sandbox. And from then on we were allies.
From skinned knees to straight skirts, from baby fat to boys, we col-
laborated on everything. At the first sign of frenzy at my house, I'd dash
up the street five doors and hang out with Lynne's family, raiding her
refrigerator for a big green Pippin apple and her closet for a new en-
semble for school the next day.

Lynne was the sister I never had.

We loved the movies and watched Debbie Reynolds sing and dance
as Molly Brown, then rescue a boat of frightened women fearing they'd
get caught in the undertow of the Titanic when it went down. We vowed
to be *unsinkable.* When she left for college two years before me, I lost
my emotional compass, and she sent me postcards of boats to remind
me to stay afloat. While dating my future mate in my senior year, she
urged me to finish my college education before considering marriage.
Sure, of course, Lynne, that's the smart thing to do. But when you're lost in
dreamland, it's easy to ignore good advice. Then my world fell apart my
first year in college when the rabbit died. In the old days, before home

pregnancy tests, this expression meant a woman was *expecting*. It was an era when an unmarried girl left town for an extended visit with "Aunt Millie" and came home a few pounds thinner.

Lynne was my Aunt Millie. She sheltered her pregnant friend in Santa Barbara and drove me to the hospital after my water broke during my seventh month. She held my hand as I gave birth to a stillborn baby girl. She brought a box of tissues I didn't need because I stuffed the pain. She was on hand when I married in haste, though I confessed nothing of my marital struggles to Lynne; she had such high hopes for me. My motto: *I will make this better by myself.*

Lynne began her teaching career, found her life mate, and welcomed two adorable daughters to her family. Our visits—because we now lived three hours apart—grew more seldom. We still called and sent cards, but those lazy days of hanging out together sipping iced tea on the patio were few.

When my marriage fell apart, Lynne was my SOS call. From her I would never hear those dreaded—though well meaning—words of my church friends, "You're better off without him." Nor the confidence crushing words, "I told you so," even though she had proposed several other options to my hasty marriage, and I chose not to listen.

She gave me what my wounded heart most needed to hear—inspired by *The Unsinkable Molly Brown*—"This is your Titanic, Jan. Don't get sucked into the undertow. Trust God and just keep rowing."

I can do that, I can put one oar in front of the other, I thought. And it wasn't too long before I found Christ and began the journey to learn what trusting God really meant as I settled into single life. I'll never forget the day Lynne phoned with the news that she had a brain tumor. "Surgery is next week," she said and we celebrated its success with a banner weekend of girl fun, and I donned a hat so we'd look like twins.

But three years later another tumor appeared, and this one was inoperable. Her husband chose to keep the truth from her—and the rest of us—wanting her last year to be a memorable one for the family. I can't fault him for it. He knows me and that I don't have a poker face. She would have guessed the truth.

By the time I heard the news, she had little time left. She first saw her pastor to make certain she was right with the Lord, then she spent days putting things in order, writing long letters to her daughters and choreographing her entire memorial service. "You'll say a few words, won't you? Tell some funny stories from our childhood. . . ." *Oh Lynne. Yes, of course.*

What would I do without my sister, my friend? Not just another loss in my life, but a big one. She'd been my rock, the wind beneath my wings. My counterbalance. Where I was flighty, she was grounded. It never crossed my mind that we wouldn't grow old together, gabbing about the way it used to be in the neighborhood, that we would never have another annual Christmas brunch. *This can't be.* There was far too much to do and say.

I still needed my big sister. And this time tears of grief came easily—for my friend's future cut short, for her husband, and for her young daughters who would never have the chance to know her as I did.

On our last day together, Lynne lay in a hospital bed in her family room, unable to see or speak, but she could still hear me and manage a chuckle. So I held her hand and talked endlessly, dragging up a lifetime of childhood memories, all the stories of our shared past: *The talent shows in my garage, our summers at the cabin, my driving lessons in your Blue Bomb, you tagging along on dates to chaperone me. And remember the time—the second time—I flunked algebra and you told me it wouldn't be the end of the world, that summer school wouldn't kill me, and that you're a good tutor? And sneaking onboard the aircraft carrier and getting all the way to the flight deck before we got caught?*

That's the one I'll tell at your memorial service. She managed a nod.

I'm glad our parents bought houses on the same street. Then I shared what she meant in my life, the example she'd been. *I can't wait to get to heaven to be with you. Have a big Pippin waiting for me.*

Her death was a defining moment that altered me forever. But I can smile each time I look at the picture of two toddlers in a sandbox, and I can still hear her whisper, "Trust God and keep rowing."

Costars: Our Bosom Friends

We all long for a friend who knows our faults and loves us anyway. In *Anne of Green Gables,* Anne Shirley is an orphan tossed from one home to another, who yearns to give up her imaginary playmates for real friends. She yearns for a "bosom" friend—an intimate friend—a kindred spirit with whom to confide the secrets of her inmost soul. It happens when she meets her shy neighbor Diana and the girls swear devotion to each other forever.

Isn't "bosom" a strange, antiquated word? No need to explain what the main definition is, but it's a picture of the safety and closeness of being held in a warm embrace. In the classic books I enjoy reading I may see "she held the sleepy child to her bosom."

Our bosom friends are the costars in our story; they are on hand during our most important scenes, the comic and the tragic. Ralph Waldo Emerson described the perfect friend as one to whom we can think aloud. And it is only through this kind of sharing that we come to know ourselves, John Powell said. "Introspection of itself is helpless. We can confide all of our secrets to the docile pages of a personal diary, but we can know ourselves and experience the fullness of life only in the sharing with another person."[1]

Friends shape who we are and who we are yet to be. According to a friendship study by University of California Los Angeles, friends soothe our tumultuous inner world, fill the emotional gaps in our marriage, and help us remember who we really are."[2] Friends are stress reducers and help us live longer. Women who lose a spouse or go through a divorce move on to their new season with more vitality if they have a close friend or two who have known the same heartbreak because they can carry each others' burdens (Gal. 6:2).

Forget fancy vitamins, go find a friend.

Sometimes when we get overwhelmed—work, family, goals—we put friendships on the back burner. We vow, "We'll get together later, when things settle down."

My junior high pal Brenda who now lives just thirty minutes away called me a while back. "Jan, I was watching this Oprah show all about the power of friendship and how it shapes our lives." She jabbered on about it, insisting that we stop making excuses and schedule our first annual girl time gathering with two other classmates. "We have to do this. We can't let any more time go by."

Amen to that. The years slipped away from Lynne and me because life got in the way. It always will. We think we'll always have tomorrow, next month, next year. But life is so short. True friendship is like sound health, said Charles Caleb Colton. The value of it is seldom known until it's lost.[3] So true, and I need to nurture ties with high school buddies like Brenda and Roanne, girls who swooned with me to the Righteous Brothers singing "You've Lost that Lovin' Feelin'." Two weeks ago—after three postponements, we met for our reunion weekend, at a women's conference where I spoke. After, we spent three hours bonding (and wrinkling) in Roanne's hot tub, running down before running out of conversation. We've shared grade school and high school, and because God is the current that surges through each of us, we relate authentically to each other now. We already have the date set for next year. True friends are slow ripening fruit and require time and patience. They're rare and should be treasured. As Oprah said on her friendship program, there are plenty of girls who want to ride with you in the limo, but a true friend is one who'll take the bus with you when the limo breaks down.

The Troupe

And then there are the stock players in your life, friends on hand for support and fun. During my single years a troupe of us hung around together, and these women became my spiritual sisters. For my bachelorette party before marrying Carl, the girls kidnapped me for a weekend in a mountain cabin. You should have seen the "outfits" they threw together when they raided my closet. Good thing they're my pals; they forgot to pack any shoes.

On our second morning, they ushered me into the living room for "testimonial" time. Jeanne and Mary Gail had cooked up an entire program where each gal shared what my friendship had meant to them. Tears flowed like a broken fire hydrant.

It was light-years away from my bowls of popcorn on the floor, six of us flopped in sleeping bags, hair jammed into curlers, playing another round of Truth or Dare. At this sleepover, I saw how much these women loved me. Me—with all my flaws and fragments. Me—who grew up distrusting females, always wondering, "What's her agenda?"

Sometimes it's simply unmasked sharing. I begin *After the Locusts* with a scene from our weekly prayer group. We've been gathering at 7 A.M. in a quiet corner of Sweet Pea's restaurant for more than fifteen years. (And yes, Popeye has his picture on the wall, too.) Many readers write me longing for this. "I wish I could find a close group of women like your prayer group." We are a troupe of six or seven most weeks. We order breakfast—the oatmeal raisin pancakes are tops—then get down to share and prayer. Nothing is sacred at that table: we expose our frustrations, fears, deepest longings, fantasies, confessions, and "think out loud" to each other. No games.

Several new ladies have visited in the last year—we are not a closed group—but none have returned. Is it their busy schedule or is it our gut-level honesty? I really don't know.

Finding a group of women to encourage can be as close as your keyboard. As an author, I live a life secluded from my colleagues, so I joined an online support group of women authors and speakers, most I've never met. But it doesn't matter. We are teamed at the heart through our ministries. We exchange tips, hints, advice, resources on writing and speaking, ask for prayer and—this is key for me—post our little bellyaches and share our sorrows because, as one sister said, "We all need a safe place to cry." Even if it's cyberspace.

My friend Cindy's posts always begin, "Dear Sisters-who-know-what-my-life-is-like." It's so true. There's nothing like a sister who knows what your life is like.

Bit Players

My past is filled with special acquaintances, coffee klatch comrades, writing buddies, small group study partners—a litany of special women who've touched and taught me. We exchange chatty Christmas letters, call once in a while to catch up, but fade into the background most of the time. Sometimes friends have only a bit part in your life—they buzz in for a few scenes, say a few memorable lines, and exit stage left. You may see them again on occasion and pick right back up where you left off.

Take Dolonda, my hairdresser, for instance. I arrived for a "trim" and left in tears. We differed on what a "trim" was, and she whacked off my hair to a more manageable length. "I'll never use her again," I mumbled, but back I came to her chop chair. Come to find out, we have similar backstories, and as we chatted, our masks fell like my mass of curls.

For many (many) years she's been cutting my hair and weaving in blonde highlights. I've watched Dolonda go from the spiritually confused to spiritually confident, from searching for a man to seeking purpose with Christ. "Think of it, Jan," she told me recently. "I have a ministry right here in this salon. I have the undivided attention of hundreds of women who are just as confused as I was and need the truth. It's so exciting, and I have you to thank for being there to listen and guide me as I sorted it all out."

Girlfriend, I am the one who's blessed.

My friendship with Dolonda taught me to "hold space for someone," as our elder chair said recently in the church service, to quit preaching and let a friend come to the truth in God's time. The old Jan couldn't wait to straighten someone out spiritually with her wealth of biblical wisdom. Again, for all the right reasons, but throwing "should's" at them is focusing on changing their outer behavior, not restoring their soul. Through my constant friendship and support, Dolonda came around to the truth in her own way, reading the Word, seeking out a Bible believing church, leading a women's recovery group. Our brief encounters every few months taught me to pray and not preach, to speak only what the Lord prompted me to say. Over time Dolonda knew all my backstory. "Really? Now I've got a question. What does God think of this . . ." she'd say. Sharing from my own experience spoke louder than any sermon.

I did nothing special, except be there and be real.

Yes, I'm the blessed one. I have a standing appointment for great girl talk and the best color and cut in town. And by the way, she was absolutely right—I look so much better with short hair.

Stumbling Blocks

When my mate walked out, I blamed "the other woman." I went ballistic, spewing out green bile of hate for the wench who stole my mate from his family. I was convinced she had seduced and bewitched him, as if he were powerless to make his own choices. Forgiving her took eons longer than forgiving him. I had quite the knack for making excuses for men and finding fault with women.

Looking back to my pigtail years, I saw that it stemmed from the mom factor. To me, my daddy was perfect and my mother the headache in the house. I resented her for the stress she caused my sweet and loving daddy. And as you know, I kept my distance from her emotionally. Whenever we have a loose connection with the first significant woman in our life, something goes missing, the crucial natural bond. When our mother rejects and hurts us—or we lose her during our critical years—it sets the tone for the way we relate to other women. Once I stopped blaming my mother for every bad decision I made in my life, I learned to accept and love her; and the walls came down with all women.

If you find that your female relationships are rocky, it may be that a breech in a family relationship is at the root. I share my mom story at every retreat. Here is Darla's* response. "Wow, I've always gotten along better with men too, and I just realized why."

And Katie* who never found a bosom friend. "I just couldn't seem to get the connection that I desired from my mother. Not until I realized that she did the best she knew how to do. That acceptance created a level of peace within myself because it freed me to stop looking for the perfect mother, and therefore the perfect friend."

True friendships involve risk, inviting another woman to see through the masks. We need friends who see through our false faces and are willing to love who we really are and help us shed the ugly stuff. A true friend will help us find ourselves. She'll laugh and cry with us and share a good chick flick. She'll encourage us to trust God and keep rowing—and growing—and stand firm for Christ.

It's been said that true friendship is mutual blackmail elevated to the level of love.[4] An open invitation to threaten each other with serious arm-twisting if we see any deception going on. Find a true friend, a sister in Christ, and agree to be accountability partners.

We are like angels with only one wing, able to fly only by embracing one another.

A true friend, a bosom friend, will carry your cue cards and whisper to you the correct lines when you start to stutter. She is your stand-in double and won't hesitate to step in for you whenever you're weak and weary. She is like Ruth with Naomi, sharing your sorrow, refusing to be sent away. "Where you go I will go" (Ruth 1:16).

And if you're really lucky—and really blessed—she'll be a Lynne.

Digging in Together

1. Read these Scripture verses relating to friendship: John 15:13; 1 Samuel 20:42; and Proverbs 18:24. Have you ever had a bosom friend? Share the qualities you most admire about her.

2. Have you had a bit-part friend who drifts in and out of your life on occasion but has added much to your life? Describe the impact that relationship has had on your life.

3. What are any stumbling blocks that keep you from *deeper friendships with women?* Are you shy? Too busy? Is it the Mom Factor?

4. Have you known a Ruth, someone you've pushed away but she refused to go (Ruth 1:16–18)?

5. Read Proverbs 27:17. How can friendship sharpen us?

Chapter 14

Cast Party

Release your playful child.

She can laugh at the days to come. (Proverbs 31:25)

When the fun of the play is over and the final curtain comes down, it's time to unwind and unravel at the cast party. After the senior high musical cowritten by me, I offered to host the cast party in our family room. We munched, chatted, reflected, danced, and joined in some silly fun, disrupted briefly by a moron who snuck in some beer and my dad tossing him out the front door.

The senior play was our swan song. We were taking our final bow, leaving the high school stage, graduating to more freedom and responsibility. We couldn't wait to grow up and venture out into the next chapter of our lives.

Years later I went to my first class reunion with hesitancy because I hadn't reached any of my dreams—to be a playwright and actress—and my marriage had just dissolved. Then I saw a familiar face at the welcome table, a grammar school classmate who smiled as she handed me a nametag with my yearbook picture pasted on it. My hair, freshly bleached Sandra Dee blonde, was ratted six inches high on my head and styled in the perfect sixties flip.

As I made the rounds, the cliques of yesteryear had vanished, save a

144

few who came with their noses slightly elevated and couldn't wait to flaunt their success. Most of us, though we spent less than four years together, felt the mysterious common bond of an experience that comes only once in a lifetime. We were there to connect with the others who had twisted the night away with Chubby Checker, who walked the institution-like halls and celebrated the miracle victories of our football team. We had come to grab a piece of the past, steal a taste of simpler times—when we were oblivious to a world exploding with civil unrest, war protesters, hippies, drugs, and free love—to recapture what had fled by at express speed without our knowing it: youth.

I'm a reunion groupie now, and often called the Perpetual Teenager. A far cry from the one who tried to mask my quirks and craziness and tried to conform to the norm. When straight hair was in I ironed my curls. All the little oddities that made me unique I attempted to cover up to fit in. And later, as a mom I insisted on wearing the mask of the right example, misunderstanding what it means. As if maturity meant mellow, controlled, and proper, and happiness was something to strive for like a university degree. Both come with facing and accepting the reality of who we really are and how we fit into the world we live and work and love in.

Once Upon a Time

Somewhere in my trek to grow up, the little girl in me got lost. Perhaps yours did too, the one who believed that pumpkins turned into coaches and if we find the magical kingdom, we'll be happy. Look at any child, and her whole world is about discovery and being in the moment. But eventually, we trade those childhood fantasies and segue into real life, getting on with the business of living with pain and disappointments and working through them. But some of us never received a script coaching us how to go from childhood to womanhood. We were into survival mode, and grew up way too soon. I remember at ten years old thinking, *I am on my own. My parents are too wrapped up in their problems.* Forced to take care of myself emotionally, I began chasing my pipe dreams. And we know where that leads.

Once upon a time all of us were young girls, but so often we let a difficult childhood interfere with us. Maybe you grew up in an angry home or were constantly criticized or expected to be perfect. Perhaps you were abused in some way, and like me at the beginning of my spiritual makeover, you now struggle with feeling your buried pain; the old feelings are dammed up behind the masks. So we grow up unsure of our true value and disown our backstory.

No, childhood was not a party for many of us. We've talked about how living the real life is dependent on sharing our true feelings and releasing the creative woman inside. My childhood makes a constant comeback in my life—and often as a conflict—but once you recognize this it cannot trip you up anymore. You may stub a toe, but you won't break a leg.

Right now, think back on your childhood, not the dark moments, but ignite your memory with thoughts of just being a little girl. Your favorite toys, dolls, friends, playmates. Did you build leaf houses in the front yard in the fall? Sand castles at the beach? Look at any child, and her whole world is about creative expression. Every day is a new beginning. You were that girl once.

It's nice to revisit your childhood firsts—when you first jumped off the high dive or rode your bike without hanging onto the handlebars. Think about lazy summers and games of hide-n-seek. I have vivid pictures of the ice cream truck rounding the corner, and I can still see all the kids scurrying home for Mom's loose change. My favorite was the Sidewalk Sundae where I could lick off all the nuts.

This month at a yard sale I bought a doll for my three-year-old granddaughter. She's as tall as Carly and has elastic straps under her shoes so you can slip your feet in and dance with her. Carrying her to the car I saw myself dancing across the floor with my own dolly years ago, imagining myself as Ginger Rogers with Fred Astaire. My eyes sparkled all the way home. When Carly arrived, she ignored my find, but who cares, the doll is just for me. She's perched on my bookshelf right now, and I still haven't stopped smiling.

When we relive childhood joys we recapture some of the little girl inside, the one who loved discovery, who didn't need to follow a script to know how to play.

Maybe that's why we love Disneyland, the happiest place on earth, they claim. For an entire day or two our only concern is being on time for our Fast-Passes, trying to fit in snacks and lunch while we are busy having so much fun. And for me, it's heading over to the teacups and riding them at least twice because they are my earliest memories of being a kid at Disneyland. And when the fireworks begin, so does our melancholy because time at the Magic Kingdom is almost over.

Of course, the responsible adult in us is relieved because it means we can stop spending money.

A child feels joy because she lives in the moment. My little granddaughter laughs at everything, and she's fearless that anything can harm her. She trusts me to catch her when she jumps off her bed or into the pool. Small children can't grasp a spiritual concept, yet by nature they trust God and people.

Feral Cats

I had watched Micki* all weekend. Her sharp wit, rough edges, and the tattoo just above the shoulder set her apart from most young mothers at the retreat. After my last presentation she chased me down to talk. We sat under a sprawling oak tree, its parched leaves announcing the end of a dry California summer, and she told me her story.

"I stopped off at Starbucks for an iced mocha," she said. "I'm out on the patio sipping my coffee and I see this cat dart out, snatching at bagel crumbs. Such a beautiful gray cat with shimmering green eyes filled with fear." Suddenly, the store owner appears. "The cat's wild, been here for weeks. I want her gone. If you'll take her, I've got a cage in the back and I'll trap her for you."

Fat chance, I hate animals, especially cats, she was about to blurt. For weeks, her kids had been begging her for a pet and Micki refused, "No way, after a month I'd be the one taking care of it." Micki's mouth opened to decline. Instead an "Okay, I'll take her," popped out. *What have I done?*

"There I am driving home with this caged cat hissing and scratching, hair flying everywhere, and I'm wondering if I'm out of my mind!" In her garage the growling feline escaped behind the washer and dryer where she stayed for three days. Her husband finally said, "Better give it up, honey. Wild cats can't be tamed. I'll trap her and take her to animal control."

"No, we can't do that," she cried. "I *won't* do that." As the moon ascended in the valley sky that night, Micki stayed up surfing the Internet typing in: *"How to tame the feral cat."* She printed out volumes of tips to try: moving the food dish further out into the garage each day until the cat felt safe to eat, wrapping her in a big towel on her lap—twice a day—increasing the minutes each time as she spoke to her softly. "I'm not going to hurt you. You are so beautiful, and you don't even know it."

By retreat time two months later, Jade, the feral cat everyone gave up on, was on her way to becoming the family pet.

Micki's eyes filled with tears as she choked, "Jan, I *am* that feral cat."

At fifteen she fled an abusive home and never looked back, living like a street orphan. "I've been fighting and scratching my way through life ever since. Erecting walls so thick nobody could break through, not even my husband. In my working with Jade, trying to win her trust, God said, 'See Micki? That's how much I love *you*. No matter how you scratch and hiss, I love you and will never leave you.' My God sees me as *beautiful* while I never did. Before Jade, I never grasped the depth of his love." A love that breaks down the walls erected in our childhood.

How many sermons do you think she heard on God's love? With assurances like, "I have redeemed you; I have summoned you by name; you are mine" (Isa. 43:1). But Micki's untamed wild side never embraced the promises for herself, the one who protected herself by being the tough girl. So the Lord sent her to Starbucks that day to tangle with a feral cat so she could see that she is God's chosen one.

To help her find the little girl lost.

I have the same hope for my Jennifer. Her sharp comments still graze my heart just a bit. "I think you're still angry at me for the past, Jenny. I can't relive those years and erase any of it, though I wish I could," I told her recently. She cocked her head and nodded. "Every time we talk, I guess I'm waiting for you to criticize me."

That's my Jenny, she pulls no punches. In my quest to tame her during her teen years I went overboard in the name of teaching. I misapplied that whole "train up a child" thing; pointing out Scripture passages, buying books and audio tapes, highlighting the *right* way to live to please God. It was my MO at the time, root cause pride/control. "Mom—I'll accept the Lord when I'm ready, and I'm just *not* ready," she'd tell me, and in her own time she went forward to receive Christ during an altar call—on a Sunday when I was out of town.

That's my Jenny.

God created her to be daring, outspoken, and flamboyant, but at thirteen, when her dad resigned as a father, she grew up and left the vulnerable girl behind. *I'll make it, I'll show him.* She's a strong woman today. Someday she'll see that while her earthly dad abandoned her, God the Father wants to bring her back to the trusting child she lost. It doesn't mean weakness, but wholeness and balance.

Admittedly, she has not fully forgiven her dad, nor fully surrendered to Christ. "I know it's up to me, Mom. I've come a long way, but I know junk is still there." And it spits out at me sometimes, but I have to remind myself she's like the feral cat who's hissing for protection. There's a feral cat in all of us, I think.

Especially when we pretend not to be vulnerable, but there's a price to pay, we lose our creativity, the playful child in us, the essence of our real spirit.

The question is, how do we live as confident women today and die to those childish expectations—those elusive pipe dreams—while holding on to the bright-eyed child?

First, like Micki, risk facing your feelings, even if they're ugly, and trust again. The Bible tells us to be shrewd as snakes and innocent as doves. Find the balance between being sensible and vulnerable. You may have been fooled and foiled—and it may happen again—but you're wiser and stronger now. You know the danger signals. Be yourself, share what's on your heart, but choose wisely who you trust with your confidences. There's a time and place to wear the mask of protection, and the same for taking it off.

After our mold lawsuit, I struggled with trust. Carl and I had been stabbed in the back by people claiming to be Christians. That's hard to swallow. We'd been naïve in many ways and needed to wise up, but not so much that we should swing over to the side of suspicion and doubt and be locked in our fears forever.

It's all about balance.

The second step to living as a confident woman is to learn to receive. You never see a child give back a gift. We women have traded a world of simple pleasures for duties and striving to be everything to everybody, and giving is what we do best.

Anna* is one of these. "I've always been a servant, looking out for others," she told me. That's an understatement. Anna reaches out to everyone she meets. She'll clean your house, cook you a meal, do your shopping. She's a born nurturer, especially with animals. When her pastor suggested to the congregation that they begin each day by asking, "How do you want me to love others today?" she found it a no-brainer. "I'm a server, that's my gift."

But for the second half of the challenge she hit a snag. "Each morning I am to ask God, 'How do you want to love *me* this day?' That's not so easy for me." As a neglected child Anna missed out on being cuddled and loved and sought affection in her boyfriend, Jack. At sixteen she was pregnant and married. A teenage marriage is hard enough without the pressure of ignoring unresolved childhood hurts. As Jack pursued a career as a police officer, the marriage was on a rocky road. "Jack's very controlling and doesn't want me out of his sight," she told our prayer group girlfriends. We often planned outings and dinner parties aside from our weekly gathering, and Jack always resisted Anna coming along.

"I learned to tiptoe around the outbursts, ignore the blame," she said. "I buried it and just went on coping, doing for others, serving my family. It never occurred to me to think of my own self-nurturing or about being loved. It just wasn't in the cards. I died to the ideal marriage long ago and resigned myself to make the best of my situation. It hasn't been a bad life, just a hard one."

But being resigned to life is never good enough for God. Her pastor's suggestion is motivating Anna to see life differently. It's not the giving that causes exhaustion and burnout, it's the lack of being filled up spiritually. "There are so many ways God reveals his love, if we wake up expecting to see it, the way a child does. That's what I'm after now."

Lord, how do you want to love me today? How do you want to use me today? What a good question to wake up with. Look at what the Bible says: "This resurrection life you received from God is not a timid, grave-tending life. It's adventurously expectant, greeting God with a childlike 'What's next, Papa?' God's Spirit touches our spirits and confirms who we really are. We know who he is, and we know who we are: Father and children. And we know we are going to get what's coming to us—an unbelievable inheritance!" (Rom. 8:15–17 MSG).

Jack's latest anger outbursts prompted Anna to call a counselor who specializes in anger issues. "Why bother," said Jack. "It's never worked before." But her experience years ago at a Christian center unlocked many truths for her, so she knows better. After avoiding it for weeks, she finally called, telling Jack, "I'm going no matter what, even for myself."

With rare confidence she told us, "I'm worth every cent it will cost." Jack agreed to go but sported the "there is nothing wrong with me, it's all in your head" mask. The counselor exposed the sham they'd been living and it blew open the cracks in the relationship. When one person in a relationship risks change it threatens the one who fears it. Status quo was not good enough for Anna now, and until Jack agreed to face his own issues, the marriage couldn't heal, so she left and moved in with a friend for a while.

Now that shook him up, and he agreed to attend Lifeskills classes, perfect for those who have childhood and relationship issues.

As of this writing, they've completed the four-month program, and things are surprisingly different. "I can't believe it. We are on our way to having the marriage we both want, for the first time. It's amazing." And better yet, Anna found the courage to leave a job with an abusive boss. She deserves more, and now she knows it.

She also understands the past is over and the future hasn't happened, so it's silly to dwell in either place. She is trying to savor each day and what it holds and to revive her childhood spirit. The difference in her is hard to miss.

Get to the "Who Cares" Stage

What's the lesson for us? We need to see life as an adventure and break out of our idea of what's "proper." To find the joy of our lost little girl we have to relearn how to play and recharge our creative batteries.

Look at the Red Hat Society ladies. This over-fifty crowd is having a jolly time wearing wacky outfits and having fun. They've gotten to the "who cares" stage, the "*so what if people think I'm crazy*" stage.

I arrived there quite by accident seventeen years ago. It was early in our singles ministry and one of the guys—Richard from the little red toolbox story—hosted a sock hop. The invitation said, "Come in fifties/sixties costumes and let's rock and roll." I offhandedly said to Jeanne, "What about doing a lip sync song?" We put out the word for back-up singers but only Julie volunteered. The three of us rehearsed "*My Boyfriend's Back, and there's gonna be trouble, hey la, hey la . . .*" in Jeanne's living room. We knew all the steps and had all the moves. By the time the party started, we looked like a sixties girl group, neck scarves, pony tails, and all.

Richard came "backstage" and asked, "How shall I introduce you?" We waved him off, who cared? So he stepped out front and said, "And now for our special entertainment, we've spared no expense to bring you the . . . Pointless Sisters."

After our three minutes of fame, a guy came up to us and said, "That was pointless, but very cool. How about performing at my fortieth birthday party next week?" We laughed, thinking he may have had too much sugar from the punch. *That was performing?* But he kept insisting it's what he wanted, so we decided, why not? We showed up with a new song—to which we rewrote the lyrics and personalized them for him—decked out in mini-skirts and go-go boots. We were so bad we were good. Three more minutes of fame, but free food and a night out.

But these boots were made for walking in a new adventure because along came more requests for the Pointless Sisters: birthdays, showers, anniversary parties, even Richard and Lorena's wedding reception. "You want us to get up there and do this in front of all your guests?"

"Of course," they answered together. "And really roast us," Richard said. You have to know their story to understand that request, and we complied.

The Pointless Sisters have tried to retire for years, but somebody has a milestone birthday or decides to get married and out comes the costume box. When Mary Gail and Hal set the date, she told us, "Now, you two are the entire entertainment. I can't afford anything legitimate."

So in tacky bridesmaid dresses from the thrift shop, we sang song parodies that made the guests laugh and Mary Gail blush. "You get what you pay for," I joked. Okay, so we got a bit carried away recapping their romance, but afterward she said, "It was so awesome."

When Jeanne and I first began the act, our Saturday night singles group was going strong. Almost every week someone would say to me, "I can't believe Christians can have so much fun." Comments came mostly from the strays, those who had been raised in the church but had drifted away and were searching to connect again. And the idea that believers can let their hair down and be silly was a new concept for them.

Our frivolity and sense of fun was the biggest attraction next to our sound biblical teaching, not to mention the two men in our leadership team—both hunks.

A while back, while flipping through the channels, I caught the end of a program, *Actor's Studio,* where Jane Fonda was the guest. As you may know, Fonda made a name for herself—aside from being Henry Fonda's daughter—as a film star in the late sixties and seventies, then with her workout videos in the eighties, not to mention as an anti-war activist during the Vietnam era.

On the program she talked about being in the third act of her life—and there is no dress rehearsal she reminded us—and found herself facing sixty finally wondering how to fill the emptiness in her spirit. Wealth, fame, and relationships never fulfilled her. Her mother committed suicide when Jane was twelve, and her father was emotionally distant. She spent her life performing, striving, seeking validation in relationships, and coming up empty.

I listened with interest when she announced that she had become a Christian, that during her search she met up with Christians who lived out their faith and were fun and hip.

I'm not sure she's found all the answers yet, but her comments that night stuck with me. *Christians who lived out their faith and were fun and hip.* Wow, that says so much. During this woman's travels, no doubt many believers witnessed to her and slipped her a few tracts with the four spiritual laws, maybe dropped books in the mail outlining the way to repent and reach heaven. But what finally attracted Jane Fonda—because she sought to reconnect with her little girl lost—was the childlike spirit she saw on believers' faces, the love of Jesus shining through them. *Fun and hip.*

Where is your little girl today? Are you looking for her, the one who laughed at the simplest things, who dared to dream, who cared less about her appearance or accomplishments than how she would chase an adventure today? The little girl who knew what she wanted to be when she grew up and imagined herself in the role? Who trusted that God would catch her and kiss her boo-boos if she fell?

It's long been said that youth is a state of mind, and the way to feel young is to keep your faith young. I wonder if this is what Jesus meant when he said, "Let the little children come to me, and do not hinder them, for the kingdom of God belongs to such as these" (Mark 10:14).

Only when we feel secure are we free to be who we really are. "See how very much our heavenly Father loves us, for he allows us to be called his children, and we really are!" (1 John 3:1 NLT).

Yes, we really are.

Digging in Together

1. As a child what was your favorite way to play?
2. What will it take for you to reconnect with the little girl in you? What can you do today that will bring back a bit of childhood joy?
3. Has God ever used object lessons like the feral cat to highlight a principle in your life? If yes, share your experience with the group.
4. Read Matthew 18:3–4 and Mark 10:14–15. What are the child-like qualities you'd like to recapture, spiritually and emotionally?
5. What holds us back from being Christians *walking in our faith who are fun and hip?* What are some ways you can incorporate more lightness, more playfulness, in your life right now?

Chapter 15

The Road Show

Hit shows always go on the road.

Wherever we go he uses us to tell others about the Lord and to spread the Good News like a sweet perfume. (2 Corinthians 2:14 NLT)

During World War II Bob Hope took his variety show on the road. A troupe of pretty gals always tagged along to remind our GIs of home and what they were fighting for. And the show, a huge morale booster, didn't stop when the war did. Hope and his gang visited military bases every Christmas until his body wouldn't cooperate anymore. *Thanks for the memories.* The USO (United Services Organization) dubbed him their "ambassador of good will."

The Bible says we are to be Christ's ambassadors, his spokeswomen, and our message for the world is nestled in our story.

Esther's story—her courage and faith that saved her people—gave birth to the yearly festival of Purim, a Jewish tradition that still celebrates God's goodness. During the dark days of World War II, the Jews needed a thread of hope to hang on to as they faced annihilation. They recalled Esther's story, and how the evil Haman hatched a plot to kill the Jews. Uncle Mordecai asked Esther to intervene to save her people. *Approach the king without being summoned? Do you know the penalty if he's not happy to see me? Death!*

Her uncle was persuasive. "Has it occurred to you that you might have

155

come to a royal position for such a time as this?" After three days of prayer and fasting Esther said, "Yes, I will go to the king, and if I perish, I perish."

She hatched a plan and outwitted Haman, saving her people (Esther 8).

To the Jewish people, Hitler was a modern-day Haman, and Esther became a symbol of hope, that God does indeed work behind the scenes preparing his people, intervening when all seems lost.

You and I may never rise to be the queen of anything, but we still have a destiny to fulfill. We come wired for a purpose. And some of us are wired weirder than others. Still, despite our age or season of life, we have been chosen to be like Esther and change our little world for the good. *If I perish, I perish . . .* really just means, *I'm your servant, Lord, and whatever you ask me to do, I'll do the right thing and trust you with the results.*

Every woman wants her life to count for something. And we try all kinds of ministries hoping to find where we fit, where we can make a difference. Carl and I teach a class on discovering your S.H.A.P.E. (Spiritual gifts, Heart, Abilities, Personality, and Experiences) and helping people identify how they are gifted to serve. When I speak to women's groups I give a pep talk on living out your God-given passions.

I read in a magazine somewhere that women share a universal longing to live with passion. We are emotional creatures who feel strongly about issues. We desperately want to invest our time and energy in pursuits that count and to find and fulfill a purpose bigger than ourselves or our problems.

Most of us go through life either not knowing we have a calling or denying its value. God went to a lot of trouble in the way he crafted us, so do we want his work to go to waste?

The Greek for the word *enthusiasm* is *en theos,* which means "with God." Basically, when we're operating in our passion, with enthusiasm, we're working with God. So find what trips your trigger and inspires you to pull an all-nighter, and you'll find the key to where you're gifted to serve God.

For me, it wasn't too far from my costume box.

So much that we do for the church is done out of guilt or obligation, not the joy of our passion. When we unleash passion, God unleashes his glory. Even the most disagreeable task can be exhilarating when it rises out of our core heartbeat and the gifts God has given. It's an invitation to get ready for new horizons and new challenges, moving into action to be effective for the kingdom of God. He calls us to live according to his purposes, to make the most out of every opportunity that comes our way. This is the key to joy in life.

We've been talking about unmasking and getting real, about touching a life with who you really are, because your transformed life is the most powerful witness.

"Those who become Christians become new persons," Paul tells the Corinthians. "They are not the same anymore, for the old life is gone. A new life has begun! All this newness of life is from God, who brought us back to himself through what Christ did. And God has given us the task of reconciling people to him" (2 Cor. 5:17–18 NLT).

So that's our task, reconciling others to him. Renewing and restoring them to their King.

Jesus lived an intentional life, to do the will of the Father (John 6:38). No more, no less. A clearly defined purpose that structured each day that he walked on earth.

I'm sure, if you're reading this book, that you don't want to be just a bit player in God's drama or even a walk-on with a few unmemorable lines. You want to play a significant role, one that will live on long after you do. *Remember her? What a legend.*

You have a legacy to leave behind.

We have no idea how unmasked honesty helps a sister, a woman who crosses our lives, who says, "That's just how I feel," and then considers the direction her life is going and decides how much she needs the living Lord. Or she decides to return to him.

A woman who has wandered from her Maker is more open to Christ when she sees him shining through imperfect women like us who don't claim to have all the answers, but are honest about who we are under the masks.

My friend Carol Kent knows what getting real is. In her book, *When I Lay My Isaac Down*, Carol is painfully real as she shares the heartbreak of a murder trial and watching her son, a naval officer with an impeccable military record, sent to prison without parole. In fear for his stepdaughters' safety he killed their father. It was the news that forever changed her life. As Carol says in the book, she now walks a path no one could have predicted, a path of unimaginable devastation. The story made the national news and became a topic of a segment on *Dateline*. At first she asked the "why" questions like we all do. Eventually she gave over the outcome of her son's life to God, *expecting* him to bring blessings out of such unspeakable circumstances.

He promises he will, and that's a message all women need to hear. "When we tell our real-life stories," Carol says, "stories of what we have encountered on the journey of life, we break down barriers and create safe places to risk revealing the truth. Intimacy springs to life when we stop hiding behind the mask of denial, embarrassment, guilt or shame."

We must be who we are. "People who have had some good days in life and people who have had some very bad days. When we've quit pretending that everything is 'fine' and life is grand. When we share our stories with each other, we find a way of relating without the facade and without the need to impress. We can just be real. This brings tremendous freedom."[1]

Carol is learning this: "I can focus the deep passions of my heart on the injustices of the world, the pain and unfairness of life, on my fears for my son, on my disappointments and unfulfilled expectations—*or* I can view my situation as a piece of a much bigger production that I am not scripting. I have the awesome privilege of playing a role in God's grand story, in a drama that does not waste sorrow. This story has a positive ending."[2]

Carol has chosen, in the midst of the awful, to seek the good. Read her book, you'll be inspired.

If you want to serve the Lord, try venturing out of the Christian cliques and live your faith in the community. Okay, I'm talking to myself here. My entire social life consists of other believers. Let's face it, we all like to hang with our own kind. My social life is filled with believers and my profession is as a Christian writer and speaker. The conferences I attend, speaking at and learning from, are hosted by Christians. That is God's call on my life right now, to inspire women to live life in the light of God's truth. Still, I need to touch nonbelievers.

"Why don't you join a local service club?" Carl asked me one day.

"Too busy," I responded. "Plate is too full."

He didn't push it, but God nudged me. As a writer and speaker how can I address the concerns of the world when I'm sequestered inside my Christian cocoon? I need to know how the pre-believer (I like that expression) sees the world. So I joined a local club last spring, a group of local businesswomen who meet at lunchtime once a week. Members of the group are some of the high powered movers and shakers in our town.

During every meeting we stand and introduce ourselves, spouting off our professions. As my turn came close I wondered, "What do I say? I'm a Christian author? I write Christian books?" I settled on "freelance writer and inspirational speaker," and a few eyebrows raised, a few skeptical glances came my way, but a few smiles too. After the meeting I left thinking, "This is going to be a challenge, Lord." Talk about incentive to keep growing my character. People who don't know Christ will be watching me.

It's not that we should wear masks and hide our faith, but these women need to know me not as *Christian* Jan—that's a label anyone can wear. I want them to see me as Jan the *Christ follower* because my life is a testimony to loving and walking with Jesus. I want them to see that I'm different and then ask me to tell my story.

For decades society has left Christians alone. Like the Persians who tolerated the Jews, they let us do our thing and discounted our impact. We were just the harmless religious right who tuned in to Dr. Dobson now and then. Ignore us and we'll go away humming a few bars of "Kumbaya." When George W. Bush was officially elected president, the issue of faith popped up everywhere. *The president says he's a Christian!* He reads his Bible every day and prays? Suddenly religion became a hot topic. And when George W. was reelected in 2004, the pundits couldn't believe the margin of victory. Christians came out in droves.

Journalists wondered, "Who are these people, these evangelicals? We'd better take some notice." This week the cover of *Newsweek* magazine caught my eye at the market. *Spirituality in America.* It said that seventy-nine percent of those polled describe themselves as spiritual and sixty-four percent as religious. Spiritual union with God is an age-old search. It takes some of us to the truth and others far from it.

People are seeking answers. And if we claim to be Christ followers, they want to know: Is this faith thing real? And we don't need to have a list of Scripture verses to rattle off to prove that Jesus is the way, the truth, and the life. Don't try to be perfect, just be you. Nobody can argue with what God has done in your life.

During my ranch years, I wrote "Country Cluckin'," a humor column for our local newspaper. Every week I shared the funny mishaps and mile-stones of rural living. My daughters, at first, thought it was cool having a local celebrity for a mom. They got a kick out of classmates saying, "I read about you today." But on occasion I would hear, "Mom—do you have to tell *that* story, about the toothpick that got jammed in my foot?"

Oh, but the hospital experience was such a hoot.

Of course I was a pre-Christian then, but fan letters arrived. "I can really relate." My funny stories brightened people's day.

I have written about my daughters and use them as examples when I speak because my faith story is so tied to theirs. I'm often asked, "Do your girls know you're telling these stories?" Oh yes. There are no family secrets left. Jennifer and Amy have both agreed, "If it helps somebody else, go for it, Mom."

God is in charge of when each story makes its debut. My friend Judi Braddy is a pastor's wife and parent of a prodigal son. She and Jim almost resigned the ministry over their wayward child, but she had no idea it would be the basis of her first book. At a writers' conference a few years back, she sat with an editor and mused, "I've always thought someone should write a book aimed at ministry families with prodigal children."

The editor stopped in mid-bite, wanting to know more, and by the end of the day Judi had an invitation to write *Prodigal in the Parsonage*. Wait, hold it! "This was my 'someday' book when there was a happy ending to my family saga." But God prompted her to write the uncol-ored truth. God gave Judi a different script than she had in mind for herself—the witty and humorous books written out of her joy—and directed her to write from her pain. "I had no idea so many other min-istry families were struggling with difficult kids. As pastors we think we have to hide that our families have flaws."

To share our stories is to invite women to freely express themselves, to embrace the truth of their own backstory, to see how their mess can become their ministry. Sharing our struggles is a service to others.

Judi takes her show on the road—literally—whenever she speaks at women's conferences and with Jim at seminars on prodigal children. "I want to give them hope in tough times, when we're between a rock and a God place."

God needs you in the grand drama of life, and there are no insignificant players. He made you for a job no one else can do. And what a privilege it is, to know that the Creator of the universe wants to involve you in his production.

Lights, Camera, Action

It's cancer. Susan was hit with the devastating news on a Wednesday, and three days later arrived for breast surgery at the hospital with a Sacramento film crew waiting. Did Susan audition for the part? Hardly. The week before, a reporter had contacted Susan's doctor, the premier cancer surgeon in the area, searching for women to interview for a feature story on breast cancer. Then Susan lands in his office, and he says, "You are the ideal candidate for this story."

Not me, she thought. Susan is the drama director at our church, but the idea of sharing with the public her private battle against breast cancer was not appealing. "And yet, I knew almost instantly that I had to do this. That is, if my kids would not object," she told me. "After all, their mother's body would be all over television. The whole thing was just too much of a coincidence. It deserved deep consideration."

The documentary was originally to follow several women from the diagnosis on, but after meeting Susan and her husband, Tim—one of our church pastors—the journalist decided she would showcase just their family, and a pastor's family at that. "That's when I knew for sure it had to be God-ordered."

Susan's story would be the spotlight story, and little did the journalist know that God would be directing it.

So it was "lights, camera, action" throughout Susan's surgeries, and the months of chemotherapy treatments, and the difficult and long recovery. The crew was on hand for Susan's first day behind the wheel of her car, her return as a proud mom to the grandstands of her kids' sports games, and the first day back at church. Ten months after her nightmare began, cameras were filming the Gregorys trimming their Christmas tree.

Hundred of thousands of area viewers heard Susan describe her cancer experience, how it made her realize that every day is a gift, and that life is so precious. Tragedy can turn into a blessing, she said, and trials serve to increase our faith.

And the God-talk was not cut from the final production. Yes, the Lord got some good press out of this one.

While her body may have been weakened with cancer, Susan's spirit had been in readiness for years for such a time as this. As a pastor's wife, Susan's prayer has always been, "God use me with my gifts and my experiences." We never know from where the casting call will come or what stage will present our story, and it may come as a shocking surprise. Once Susan knew this opportunity was clearly from God, she ignored the inner voices of fear and the practical disruptions it would bring to her life and obeyed out of devotion to the Lord.

"I didn't ask for the cancer," Susan said in the documentary. "I didn't expect it, but I'm expecting to grow through it and to glorify God."

One of our church members works for our local public television station, and she produced a documentary on breast cancer highlighting Susan's story too. Both shows won regional Emmy awards and are continuing to air all over the state and beyond as I write this.

What a legacy. Susan's story is a gift of hope for other women who may be faced with the worst shock of their life. "They can look for the good in it and find it."

Shakespeare said, no legacy is so rich as honesty.[3]

Digging in Together

1. If you were asked to be in a television documentary sharing your crisis, like Susan's cancer journey, would you decline politely, agree reluctantly, or jump at the chance to have your story told?

2. How would you write the epitaph on your tombstone? What words would you use to reflect your life's purpose? For what do you want to be remembered?

3. In the parable of the talents (Luke 19) Jesus says we are accountable for what we are given. What gifts and talents do you have that can be used more effectively?

4. What parts of your story are you ready to share with others to bring glory to God?

Chapter 16

Blockbuster

Your story is a smash hit every time.

Arise, shine, for your light has come, and the glory of the LORD rises upon you. (Isaiah 60:1)

She calls herself the former "iron woman." We first met at a holiday tea. "I'm Jeffry—yes, that really is my name," she said. "I've read your book, and I have a story to tell you." Intriguing words for any author. We met a few days later over Chinese food. Sipping a bowl of steamy won-ton soup, she started in about her journey to wholeness.

But, wait, hold on, first things first. Inquiring minds have to know: *How did you get your name?* "My parents thought I would be a boy and since they were bonded to the name, it stuck. So I'm Jeffry," she said in a way that told me she liked it.

After talking for an hour, I said, "Women need to hear your story, Jeff, have you ever thought about speaking?" *As a matter of fact . . .* she told me God had been prompting her recently. So last spring—after a little coaching—she made her debut at a local ladies night out, and I came to cheer her on. "Go ahead and critique me," she said. "I want to learn to do this." As an artist, she communicates through the visual and brought with her as illustrations, her paintings.

She began her talk by placing on an easel the painting of a woman with a metal mask hinged to her face. "Here is a self-portrait of me. I wore a mask of the iron woman, hard on the inside, and so self-sufficient. A woman who could accomplish everything, who thought it was her responsibility to do it all. People saw me as a happy person and content, a woman who thought she knew God, but behind the mask were very toxic thoughts. Sharing my honest feelings was never natural for me. As a wounded child growing up without a father, I shoved my feelings under the rug."

As she removed the mask from the painting we saw underneath an innocent girl with childlike faith. "But I drifted away from God, never fully understanding his character. My ears had distorted the truth of who the Lord is." Jeff had been married for more than a decade and was a mom before she began searching for her spiritual roots. "I made a commitment to Christ and joined a local church. My marriage with Greg looked good on the outside, but as I explored Christianity the cracks in our relationship widened. Continual strife. I felt isolated and all alone."

Then Satan came on the scene as he often does to lure a new believer from God's heart. "A man at church showed me attention and gave me compliments. I thought, 'Here is a Christian man who sees value in me that my husband doesn't.' I desired to be swept off my feet, and he was more than willing. First Corinthians 10:13 says that God is faithful and he won't let you be tempted beyond what you can bear. So true. The Lord kept showing me ways out of this dangerous attraction—we were friends, no big deal, so I thought—but I ignored the danger signs, preferring to justify that this must be from God because, *I'm not happy at home.*"

Doesn't God want me to be happy? she wondered. Oh, and don't we invite trouble when we say that?

Through weekly Bible studies Jeff found out who her heavenly Father really is and that his plans for his daughters are better than the ones we design. Soon after, Greg got wind of the affair. "He got angry and threatened to leave," she said. "Ah ha, this is my way out, I thought. He'll be leaving me, so it's not my fault."

Bring on the wrestling match: Jeff and God in a match of wills. "I wasn't practiced in hearing from the Lord yet, but I cried out to him in my confusion and pain, telling him, 'I don't understand any of this, but I need you.'" Like me, Jeff's image of God was warped. "I thought he was punishing and cruel, that he wanted me to sacrifice what I really wanted—true love and happiness—and give up my dreams."

She had no hope. *Lord, I don't deserve this marriage struggle. Is this my cross to bear?* "Still, I knew that if I wanted a relationship with God, I couldn't stay this way, clinging to a wrong relationship. I learned that obedience is God's will for me, that despite my feelings he wanted me to give up my own desires and surrender to him. Painfully, I cut off the relationship, and my husband decided to stay and work out our differences."

Fortunately, Jeff had a supporting player, her best friend Debbie. "I risked telling her all my toxic thoughts about my life and my mate. I thought she might run from me, but Debbie never said a condemning word, she cried with me and said that she loved me, and God did too. I'd never known that kind of unconditional love before."

A bosom friend is crucial for helping us make the right decisions.

Jeff wondered, can God forgive the iron woman and all the crud she's hidden for so long? Her journey to wholeness began with a tiptoe. "And I saw that God doesn't hand down a list of 'to dos' because he's a dictator, but because they are changes we need to make for our own good, that he has a plan for us, like it says in Jeremiah 29:11, for a future and a hope. My marriage was so painful, I wondered if I could hang in there to see it through." As an illustration she brought out the next painting. "This was me, clinging to a vine that looks pretty but is withering away. We cling to our old beliefs and our toxic feelings that we're afraid to share with anybody. Once we do share them, they begin to dissipate and lose their power.

"I learned there are no perfect people, and I no longer had to put on this facade and guard my heart. It was a time of self examination. Okay, I'm miserable in my life, and I have a choice—continue on my own or do it God's way. And that means letting people in, sharing my feelings, becoming the real me.

"This was the most painful and difficult thing I had to do. You see, I was raised always to do the right thing. I'd spent my marriage wearing the mask of self-sacrifice, playing the role of the dutiful wife, trying to please him and gain acceptance from my family, resenting it all the way."

Jeff had to discover what honesty is. "Before I revealed myself to my husband I practiced with Debbie, pledging to hide nothing from each other. Slowly I learned to say, 'No, I'd rather not,' and it was okay. She wasn't going to leave the friendship. This gave me confidence."

Still, she struggled to forgive her husband for past hurts. "I learned through my marriage struggles that forgiveness isn't always for the other person, it's for us to cleanse our soul."

As she opened up to Greg, the barriers came down. "My trust grew that the Lord had a better plan for our marriage than we ever thought."

Jeff rehearsed *moment by moment* surrender. "I never understood the Bible when it talked about dying to self. I thought it was self-sacrificing, just surrendering to everybody else's whims, to keep the peace. Putting all your own needs aside, but that isn't it at all. It's really trusting him with everything, daily. Over time God removed all my masks, my perfectionism, my efforts to be good, to be in control of my own life."

Jesus always surrendered to his Father's will, she said, and he surrendered for us. "It sounds weird, but I'm grateful for the way I stumbled because it revealed how much I needed Jesus."

The next painting on display was one she painted of our Savior. "When I was walking through forgiveness I painted this picture of Jesus. The nails you see pierced through the canvas are symbols of my sins, piercing through Jesus' heart. And these teardrops, they're because he cries for us, not in pity but in understanding."

Over time the marriage mended. "We rediscovered each other and our love, and we started facilitating marriage classes at church, sharing our experiences in putting the broken pieces back together. As a team we served the Lord and our parenting became more effective. Two years after I'd almost thrown my marriage away, I thought, 'I love this man now. Can life get any better?'"

That's when she heard the news that changed everything. "I found out I had malignant melanoma that had spread to my lymph nodes."

The room quieted as Jeff shared about her cancer. "The doctors told me it was so far advanced there was nothing they could do. We were in shock for days, and I cried many grieving tears and wrestled with God until I was weary. But then my training in *moment by moment surrender* kicked in. God has been and always will be in control. I could rest in that. I prayed for my daughters. 'I'm okay, Lord. I've come to a place of peace about this, but what about them? Will this turn them into bitter women, like I once was? Will they misunderstand your character like I did?'"

One morning she read Isaiah 61 about comforting all who mourn. You "bestow on them a crown of beauty instead of ashes, the oil of gladness instead of mourning, and a garment of praise instead of a spirit of despair. They will be called oaks of righteousness, a planting of the LORD for the display of his splendor" (Isa. 61:3). "It was a promise for me for my children, that they would grow up strong, praising God. And someday people will see how he is real in their lives."

But how would she tell them? As it turned out, she didn't have to. Her nine-year-old asked her, "Mommy, are you sick?"

"Yes, Jordy, I am. I have cancer and I will probably die sooner than other mommies."

Jordy pondered it for a moment and grinned. "If you have to go to heaven, there must be a little girl who needs you more than I do."

Out of the mouths of babes. "That spoke to me so clearly," Jeff said. "They may go through some hard times, but my girls will be okay." A few days later, Jordy ran into her mother's arms. "Mommy, I'm going to miss you if you die." Cuddling close, she allowed her daughter to just feel the feelings. "Everything inside me wanted to promise her it would be fine, but words would have diminished her pain. A few minutes later she ran out to play."

We put so much weight on what we do and say, but God asks us to simply be there for people, she said. "Jesus was a man of great sorrow and great joy. He expressed it all openly. If I've learned anything it's to just be real. That's the greatest gift we can give another."

Her cancer seems to be in remission, but doctors are not optimistic, yet. And Jeff is not in denial about the sadness of her situation. "I do feel the pain of it. At Christmas it hit me, this might be the last one with my family."

Meanwhile Jeff shares her message whenever the opportunity arises. "Jesus doesn't promise to change our circumstances. He promises to give us strength and peace. Strength is not having a perfect life and peace is not the absence of pain. It's the absence of anxiety."

Will God heal Jeff or take her home to heaven? "Somehow, it's not the point anymore," she says. "Only my process and what he chooses to do with it in the meantime counts. And, strange as it sounds, it's become the biggest blessing in my life."

All the while Debbie has had a front row seat to view her best friend's story, and it's brought her into a deeper relationship with Christ. When I first met Debbie at the State Capitol, God's purpose for her life was far from her focus. And now, it's her consuming passion. Recently, she wanted to know from Jeff, "If you could change all this, would you take away your cancer?"

"You know, it's odd, but I don't think I would. Sure, my common sense tells me I need to be here to raise my daughters, but my spiritual sense says; *be concerned with just today* and trust that God knows what's best. It's true for all of us. We have an inheritance to share in his glory."

And it's our true calling.

Last week Jeff called me. "Jan, I'm still so uneasy about speaking—I like to talk but I'm no polished speaker. I was ready to give up the whole thing, then I gave a talk at a nurse's group about being a cancer patient, and you should have seen how natural I was, how effortlessly the words flowed. But with Christian groups, I'm so awkward and stiff. I wonder why."

I chuckled and told about my poor speaking start, the pressure to say all the right Christian things, and what a flop it turned out to be. And when I gave up trying to be the polished presenter, it changed. Now I'm the "come as you are" gal. I come flexible and willing to let the Holy Spirit take over. I gave her the Oswald Chambers cheer, "You are the message, Jeff. You know your material, it's your story, from the depths of your soul. Tell it your way and stop worrying whether you have the prerequisite number of Scripture passages and hit all the fine points."

"Oh, Jan, that's just what I needed to hear."

Don't we all? *You are the message.*

Back in act 2, we discussed how we all seek transformation. Life is full of glitches that force us into adjusting our old habits, patterns, responses. And God says to us, if you stay in your mess and work through it, I can guarantee you one thing, you will change and grow and discover what you've been searching for.

Real change is becoming who we are, not trying to become what we are not. And we change and grow until the last day we live.

Jeff's script isn't one we'd knock ourselves out to audition for; most of us give a secret sigh of relief when we get passed up for the big tragedies. But the question remains, if we do get the unexpected call, "Are you ready?" could we say, "Yes, Lord"? Through our tears and fears could we agree with his timing and his choice, because we know we belong to him?

The word *orphan* has come up a few times throughout this book. In Esther's story, and the feral cat. Haven't we all felt like that a time or two, confused, lost, misplaced? The Hebrew term *yatom,* one who has become fatherless, refers to those needing mercy and compassion.

Exactly what Sarah C. wrote to me about just last month. As a professional actress she makes her living being somebody else. "I think it came from being a dreamer, wanting to escape my life." She's spent the last few years deeply in love with a noncommital man. "Foolish, I know, and now he's breaking it off, and I find myself putting on the face of indifference and toughness for acquaintances, so no one will know how much I hurt. I feel like an orphan, so very much alone. My mother and best friend died of breast cancer two years ago, and my father's never been around."

Jesus used the word orphan symbolically, promising his followers, "I will not abandon you as orphans—I will come to you. In just a little while the world will not see me again, but you will. . . . When I am raised to life again, you will know that I am in my Father, and you are in me, and I am in you" (John 14:18–20 NLT).

I wrote to Sarah and thanked her for being so real. Her next e-mail said, "At this point in my life I need to hear stories of women who stepped out in obedience and were blessed with restoration."

There are many, just like Jeff's, that highlight one of God's recurring themes: He loves orphan girls. He can do a whole lot more through a wandering waif with a ready heart than a warrior woman clutching the reins of her life. His greatest desire is that we wake up each morning with wondrous expectation for what he will do through us today. And an immediate nod when we sense him saying, "I need your talents and gifts for this small role. Are you available?"

Oh, yes Lord, I was born to do this.

Digging in Together

1. Do you believe you have a role to play to bring glory to God through your life? What can God say to the world through you right now?

2. Which of the real stories in this book have touched you the most?

3. Of the Bible women we've met, with whom do you most relate: Esther the orphan, Esther the queen, Esther the spiritually single, Ruth a faithful friend, the Samaritan Woman at the well and her secrets, the Samaritan woman set free, Priscilla in her mobile tent, Lydia the entrepreneur and hospitality hostess, or Deborah the strong leader? All these women were positioned by God to be in the right place at the right time and he used their uniqueness.

4. What is the most unique thing about your personality? How might God want to use this?

5. After this time of study together, how close are you to celebrating God's goodness and the gifts he offers, to understanding the fullness of life?

Encore

Take a Bow for Jesus

Well done, good and faithful servant! (Matthew 25:21)

Who is the director's ideal actress? The one who comes to her audition ready for the role, wholly committed to giving her best for the grand production. And if she doesn't land the part she seeks, she'll take any role, large or small, because she knows:

> All the world's a stage,
> And all the men and women merely players:
> They have their exits and their entrances;
> And *one [woman] in her time* plays many parts.

Many scenes have already come and gone. Some defining and memorable. Others long forgotten. One year she's cast in a drama, the next a comedy. She's had her smash hits and flops, she's played to sell out crowds and an audience of one.

In each case she is still the star of God's heart.

She arrives at the theater every day donning her good attitude. She is done making excuses and blaming others for her failures. She owns her past and won't let it sabotage her performance. She is aware that those watching in the audience search for ways to relate to her character, and

171

the best actor is one who is identifiable and real, whose struggles are every woman's story.

At the end of the show, there is cheering and clapping and shouts of "encore." *Yes, give us more.* And our lady takes her bow, then another and another. Joy floods her soul. She takes a bow for Jesus, for this is her destiny.

Cue Cards for God's Leading Lady

Make God the consuming passion in your life.

Believe you were created in his image, that he has a role for you to play in the drama of life.

Invite him to unmask you. Show your true face to the world.

Get rid of your props. Break out of the old ways of thinking, hiding, coping. Find the little girl lost.

Seek balance. Know your limits and when you need to rest your soul and hear God's whispers.

Turn your pain into passion and your messes into ministries. Go on the road with the story of your life and share it with those who need to know that God is the answer. God is enough.

Live in the now.

Enjoy life to the fullest. Three cheers for the Lord!

Endnotes

Chapter 1: Charades and Masquerades

1. Ashleigh Brilliant, *Appreciate Me Now and Avoid the Rush* (Santa Barbara, Calif.: Woodbridge Press, 1981), 55.
2. "Material Girl Goes from Madonna to Esther," at http://www.msnbc .msn.com/id/5234922/ (June 14, 2004).
3. Beth Moore, *Believing God* (Nashville: Broadman and Holman, 2004); book review adapted from *Home Life Magazine* at www.Lifeway.com.
4. William Shakespeare, *As You Like It*, 2.7.139.

Chapter 2: Backstory

1. C. S. Lewis, *The Problem of Pain* (London: Collins, 1940), 81.
2. Carol Kent and Karen Lee-Thorp, *Six Essentials of Spiritual Authenticity* (Colorado Springs: NavPress, 2000), 6.

Chapter 3: The Casting Call

1. Winston Churchill, BrainyQuote at www.brainyquote.com (accessed June 25, 2005).

Chapter 4: Competing for the Role

1. Brenda Waggoner, *The Velveteen Woman* (Colorado Springs: Chariot Victor, 2002), 57.

2. Oswald Chambers, "Being an Example of His Message," in *My Utmost for His Highest* (Grand Rapids: Discovery House, 1935), March 10.

Chapter 5: Classical Tragedy

1. John Greenleaf Whittier, WorldofQuotes.com at http://www.worldofquotes.com/index.php (accessed June 28, 2005).

Chapter 6: Pipe Dreams

1. Carol Abaya, "The Sandwich Generation," *Sacramento Bee,* June 12, 2005.

Chapter 7: Stage Fright

1. Tracy Quinn, ed., *Quotable Women of the Twentieth Century* (New York: William Morrow, 1991), 92.
2. Leslie Ann Gibson, comp., *The Woman's Book of Positive Quotations* (Minneapolis: Fairview Press, 2002), 448.
3. Ibid., 476.

Chapter 9: The Mimic

1. Quoted from Barbara Curtis's Web site: www.barbaracurtis.com.
2. Barna Group, "Seven Paradoxes Regarding America's Faith," at www.barna.org, December 2002.
3. Tracy Quinn, ed., *Quotable Women of the 20th Century* (New York: William Morrow, 1991), 31.
4. Barna Group, as quoted on www.mcjonline.com/news (accessed March 2005).
5. Joe Baltake, review of *King Arthur* as excerpted from www.sacticket.com (July 2004).
6. Ibid.
7. Carolyn Mahaney, "Femininity: A Biblical Perspective," at www.sovereigngraceministries.org (accessed August 2005); adapted from Nancy Leigh DeMoss, ed., *Biblical Womanhood in the Home* (Wheaton, Ill.: Crossway Books, 2002).

Chapter 11: The Understudy

1. Brenda Waggoner, *The Myth of the Submissive Woman* (Carol Stream, Ill.: Tyndale House, 2005), 79.

2. Oswald Chambers, "Moral Dominion," in *My Utmost for His Highest* (Grand Rapids: Discovery House, 1935), April 12.

Chapter 12: Balancing Act

1. Leslie Ann Gibson, comp., *The Women's Book of Positive Quotations,* (Minneapolis: Fairview Press, 2002), 507.
2. Biography text for the "Unsinkable Molly Brown" program as found at accweb.itr.maryville.edu/schwartz/molly-brown.htm (accessed June 28, 2005).
3. Joanna Weaver, *Having a Mary Heart in a Martha World* (Colorado Springs: Waterbrook Press, 2000), 7.
4. Eugenia Price, *The Burden Is Light! Early Will I Seek Thee* (Westwood, N.J.: Revell, 1955), 116.
5. Ibid.
6. The Catholic Community Forum, "Patron Saints Index: Teresa of Avila," at www.catholic-forum.com (accessed June 28, 2005).
7. William R. White, *Speaking in Stories: Resources for Christian Storytellers* (Minneapolis: Augsburg, 1982), 90.

Chapter 13: Supporting Players

1. John Powell quotation found at www.habits-of-mind.net (accessed August 25, 2005).
2. Gale Berkowitz, "UCLA Study on Friendship Among Women," www.anapsid.org.
3. John Q. Baucom, *Little Baby Steps to Happiness* (Lancaster, Pa.: Starburst, 1996), n.p.
4. Robin Morgan, *The Women's Book of Positive Quotations,* comp. Leslie Ann Gibson (Minneapolis: Fairview Press, 2002), 79.

Chapter 15: The Road Show

1. Carol Kent, *When I Lay My Isaac Down* (Colorado Springs: NavPress, 2004), 175.
2. Ibid. 165.
3. William Shakespeare, *All's Well That Ends Well,* 3.5.

Recognize that sexuality is a stronghold. Ask God what He wants me to do. (attention seeking) self seeking "Doing it" for myself.